CONFESSIONS OF A

Frustrated
Business Woman

A Sixty-Day Journal to Freedom

LOUISE PLANT

BALBOA.
PRESS

A DIVISION OF HAY HOUSE

Balboa Press books may be ordered through booksellers or by contacting:

Balboa Press
A Division of Hay House
1663 Liberty Drive
Bloomington, IN 47403
www.balboapress.com
1 (877) 407-4847

Because of the dynamic nature of the Internet, any web addresses or links contained in this book may have changed since publication and may no longer be valid. The views expressed in this work are solely those of the author and do not necessarily reflect the views of the publisher, and the publisher hereby disclaims any responsibility for them.

The author of this book does not dispense medical advice or prescribe the use of any technique as a form of treatment for physical, emotional, or medical problems without the advice of a physician, either directly or indirectly. The intent of the author is only to offer information of a general nature to help you in your quest for emotional and spiritual well-being. In the event you use any of the information in this book for yourself, which is your constitutional right, the author and the publisher assume no responsibility for your actions.

Print information available on the last page.

ISBN: 978-1-5043-1400-8 (sc)
ISBN: 978-1-5043-1401-5 (e)

Balboa Press rev. date: 08/07/2018

Day 1

Dear Diary,

This diary is my journal and confessions about being a frustrated business woman.

I am writing this journal or diary because I have had enough of being another friggin unsuccessful business statistic and a woman running another little hobby business, rather than a successful, growing, exciting and expanding business.

I have written my way out of other holes so I am going to write myself out of this one as well.

I choose to commit to sixty days of writing about my wimpy frustrating business.

I will write about how it feels, what I want, what I need. In fact I'll write anything about my business.

Why am I doing this?

For now I can give you two reasons, though I am sure that over time, there will be many more.

The first reason is that I have been self-employed for thirty years or so and I have had business successes and failures. I have had enough of just being sustainably successful. I am so done with being just okay.

1

I want fantastic, exceptional and profitable success. This means that okay can just buzz off.

The second reason is that on the back of my toilet door, I have printed out inspiring words, phrases, affirmations and quotes that I read when doing other more personal business.

I put something new up there last week about self-confidence, which I had not read for months. I read it yesterday and it said to spend thirty minutes a day focusing on the person you want to be.

I believe in the law of attraction and I know that it works. My toilet reading inspired me to embark on this sixty day journey to see what I can learn.

In full disclosure, I'm writing this, for myself with the possible added intention to benefit others in similar positions. I want an exceptional business or nothing at all. This is what I want. I do not want to settle for being okay, or having money trickling in. I want to have the lifestyle and choices I dream of.

I could go and get a 9 - 5 job and just accept my lot. But that is not something I want to do. It's not who I am. I find it soul destroying. I like being an entrepreneur or an infopreneur as I call myself.

Perhaps I just need to accept my feelings and that I AM enough. Who knows?

One purpose of this dairy to explore my beliefs, habits, patterns and behaviours about my business and how I love to live it, run it, explore it and express it.

I know I have enough and I have something of value to give to those who come to me or are around me.

Nevertheless, who knows? I know that there is so much more out there, however I have to be the one who knows and believes this.

I know I love to write. And I love to teach, so that is what I will do.

I also read something else this week that asked 'What three unique things do you do?' I couldn't answer because I didn't know.

It is time to explore my life and delve into my business and what drives it.

I have no idea where I am going at this point in my life when it comes to my business, though that's not an issue.

What is an issue is my desire for more than just okay. I have the desire for feeling and being bloody fantastic.

But I digress. This is a diary after all.

Currently I am on a train. With the typical majority of the population on their phones, everyone is locked into the bondage of their screens. There is not a hint of interaction, just the flicking of touch screens, people swiping up, down, left or right. Everyone is consumed in their own worlds. So am observing this and during the next sixty days I will put my pen to paper and share my life's ventures and journey over the next two months, with the major focus being on my business.

My train ride is taking me to the city for a course I am taking and I do not know why. I am still searching for that why.

I want to know what my unique selling point is. I want to know what is unique about me. I know I have many unique qualities. There can seem to be so many of them that I do not know what the umbrella uniqueness is that covers them all. I would like more clarity and more answers and I know this diary will uncover some of them.

I want success. I want freedom. I want travel. I want to stop this overwhelming feeling I have of being frustrated, skint, and a failure. I want to feel fabulous instead. I want to not keep jumping from one shiny object to the next.

I will sit in my business space, to own it, step into it and accept where I am.

In this diary I will state the day and time and I know from past journaling that writing is a great way to shed light on things, to express oneself, to allow the creative juices and energy to flow.

That is all for now.

8.45 P.M.

I have had such an eventful day. I feel so different from how I was feeling this morning.

I learnt what my natural gifts are today and that I have four major gifts. These gifts are innately in us and are the very things that make our soul sing, bring passion into our lives and is almost like us following our true purpose.

My four gifts are writing, cultural integration, teaching and evangelism. These are my primary gifts.

This makes so much sense to me as I love to speak and write. I think this is why I like writing my wimpy diaries and journals, they are very cathartic and healing. This is good confirmation to do this venture and keep writing my confessions of a frustrated business woman.

I know this new knowledge has made me start to think. Now that could be dangerous! I know a good way to change any current situation is to put energy into what new things that I want. I am going to do this regularly through this diary. It will be a bit like dreaming about the life and lifestyle that I truly want.

I am going to write down my dream life of being a successful businesswoman.

So what I will do is to keep writing about my future and what it is that I would like to see happening, how it feels, what I am doing, hearing, experiencing and to really get a taste of what this future life will be like.

So let's start.

I will step into my life in five years in the future as a successful business woman and I will imagine what my life will be like in the future.

In five years ....

I will look so hot. I will have my own seamstress or tailor who will make suits that I love to wear and that make me feel sooo good when I have them on.

I look hot because I have more time. I have time and the financial freedom to go home and relax when I need.

I have weekly massages, regular healing sessions and even facials and natural beauty treatments. I have time and money to pamper myself and I look damn good.

As well as looking hot I also have my team around me.

They make me magical breakfasts packed full of nutrients. Organic berries, caramelised buckinis, coconut yoghurt, sliced banana, slivered almonds, and a little coconut sugar. All made especially for me.

They make it ready with a fresh organic juice, which they will always insist that I eat and drink. This is fabulous as I can easily get lost in the business of the day.

They also create my super smoothie blend for the day and hand it to me to drink. I love my team. I love how they support me in my health and wellbeing, knowing this is of vital importance to me.

A platter of organic fruit is prepared by our wonderful organic superfood caterers. This is available for us all to eat all day. Yum.

I feel great starting my day this way. I love being pampered and therapized on a regular basis. It feels great having people around me who really care for my health and welfare and want the best for me. I gratefully return that, as I truly want the best for them as well. We all mutually benefit.

How else will I spend my working days?

I have a warm spot to create and write with a fabulous view of nature. This is where the sun shines and the birds are singing. I love it when my friends the birds, come and say hello to me in the morning. This is our morning routine. The birds and I make ourselves happy. They get some healthy breakfast too and I get to hear them sing their joy.

It is good to picture my future space and focus my intention. It makes me feel good and it puts out energy for my future goals. I will spend time writing about my future. What I will explore what I will look like, be like, dress like and feel like.

This is an interesting exercise that will help me further my business future and as I write about it I will have it documented here in black and white.

Will it come true?

Who knows?

Does it matter?

No it doesn't matter. I am not doing this for a desired outcome.

I know the benefits of being grateful for what I have. This is a bit of an experiment really and I will show my excitement towards what it is that I want and desire in life.

I now feel a lot better than I did this morning. Before I felt lost and without hope. I am so sick of not having the money and the choices to do what I truly want.

This afternoon I feel like I have more direction, which is good.

I believe that I either want to be remarkable or nothing at all. It's a bit like my life. Go hard or go home.

I have been pondering over what is my message to the world as I want a message that sits right with me. I would like to spread this message.

My message is that we all have the power to heal ourselves. We also can manifest instantaneously. I believe that we have the ability to go from being f**ked to finding freedom, simply and easily if we choose. It is all a matter of time, focus and action.

I like this message. I believe that this is remarkable and it is exactly what I am looking for.

Day 2

It is not so cold today.

How is my business being frustrated and wimpy today?

I have $83 in the bank and I have to pay a bill for $113, so that will make life interesting.

I transferred $150 from my PayPal account over to the business account, so hopefully this is how I can soon pay this bill.

This is sort of how I have been living. How does the saying go, 'hand to mouth, robbing Peter to pay Paul,' something like that?

I had a little herb order come in, as I sell herbs online as well as doing many other things. That herb order came to $63 which might go through on Monday as well.

I think it would be a good idea if I will write about my financial status. I want to be transparent and also because I have to be honest about where I am.

I spent the money in my purse, so I have $150 + $83 = $233 dollars, minus $113 to come out which leaves $123, then on Tuesday I have $53 coming out, which gives me the grand total of $70 for food and other stuff for the week. $70 to feed a family is stressful and hard.

This is how I have been living and I am sick of it.

I know that there can be obstacles that can block a successful business from thriving. I have been studying business mastery the past twelve months and have been learning a lot.

I created a list and it is a handout that I give to my coaching clients. I call it my Seventeen Steps to Business Success.

I know that when I am in a certain space I find business just comes in. In ten days I earnt over $3,000 and I did it easily. I can happen. Part of this journey with writing this diary is to get to the bottom of this.

Anyway. Here are my Seventeen Steps to Business Success.

Seventeen Steps to Business Success

We all have blocks and locks that stop us from moving through our doorway to success.

Explore these locks and see which of these locks you have to unlock to walk into your world of success.

The analogy here is that you have a door to success and there are seventeen locks on it.

For us to succeed we need to have all these blocks unlocked. Just one item being locked will keep the door to success closed.

1. **The need to be liked.** We all need to be liked and we can do things so that we can be liked, though does it benefit our business success? What stops you moving forward, making those calls, making those changes? Is there a need to be liked? Are you pleasing others, rather than pleasing yourself?
2. **You time.** Alone time and space to allow your desires and ambitions to flourish is vital. For us to create we have to have the space to do so, energy has to flow. Is your house cluttered? Do you feel you have a space that you can call your own? Do you have a sacred and special healing and growing place? If you do not have a space, create one NOW.
3. **A supportive environment.** Do you have peers who tell you "You can do it!"? Are you surrounded with loving,

supportive and helpful people? If you are not then it may be time to change your environment or choose to bring a new more supportive group of peers and friends into your life?

4. **Facing your fears**. Are you avoiding what you most need to confront? You know what this is and yet you are still doing it. Our fear can leave us immobilised and paralysed. There are many ways to face our fears and one of those ways is to 'Just Do It.'

5. **Being Healthy**. Do you have a vibrant, energised, fit and healthy body? Most successful people focus on their fitness and health, as they know a healthy body, gives us a healthy focus and happiness. A healthy body is a less stressed body.

6. **Mentor.** Do you have a mentor who has done what you want to do and can guide you to achieve that? Having a mentor means you can get the work done in half the time. It means you are investing in yourself and your personal growth. It means that you are important and are validated.

7. **Consistent leads.** Do you have a stream of consistent leads of the right people coming to your door? If not, is it a mindset problem or a maths problem? Are you connecting to others or not?

8. **A clear message**. Do you have a clear and passionate, focused vision? Is it an attractive marketing message? Does it excite you?

9. **Freebies**. Do you have an exciting and valuable free offer that will give value to others? Is it something that will demonstrates what you do and will get them walking in the door?

10. **Pitching**. Are you able to pitch the right offer to the right person at the right time? Do you know when the right person or the right time is right in front of you?

11. **Confidence.** Are you confident on how you can solve their problem and help them to get what they want? Do you have an understanding of their urgent pain? Can you ethically

and confidently share the knowledge that their pain is greater than your solution?

12. **Follow up.** Do you have the commitment to follow up with calls and leads?

13. **Your offers.** Do you have enough offers to give? Are you clear on your services?

14. **Close the deal.** Are you able to close the lead?

15. **Mindset.** Do you have the belief and mindset that you have value to offer the world and to your clients? Can you see your value and how it is actually helping people and not just making sales?

16. **Alignment.** Do you meditate and practice presence? Do you know when you are aligned or not?

17. **Ongoing tweaking**. Are you constantly tweaking of yourself and your offerings so that they get a more consistent and bigger results for you and your clients? Are you collecting data, testimonials and leads?

When I first learnt about this list I had six blocks.

At the very moment of writing this I believe I have two blocks stopping my success. Success does take dedication, focus, consistency, practise and work.

It does not have to be hard. It can be easy and enjoyable.

I hope this diary will unlock the last ones of those, as I have worked hard the past two years, studied many programs and numerous courses on building tribes, public speaking, launching programs, sales, marketing, creating your vision, exploring your avatar's, and so on.

So part of the reason why I am writing this is that I am an amazing teacher, writer, facilitator, healer, therapist, herbalist, nutritionist, coach who is highly qualified, has lots of skills, abilities, expertise and qualifications and still has many frustrations around money and business.

Are you getting the picture?

You can see why I have to find a solution to this. I have been self-employed for about thirty years and my business has been an up and down ongoing journey.

There have been failures, huge debts almost to bankruptcy. This brought huge stress, a marriage break up and great instability and fear.

This has been playing out on and off all my life. Having said that, I have never invested into myself as much as I have the past two years and I think this has been a huge turning point as I have some clarity and understanding now.

To be brutally honest, it does not matter whether you understand, it is important that I understand and acknowledge where and what has been happening in my life.

I know you cannot see my situation, though some of you may resonate with it. I write this to help me to overcome my frustrations.

I think it would be good to do a daily tally of my bank situation to get real with my situation. I cannot change it until I can see where I am at.

Day 2 looks like this - $83 in bank and $150 in PayPal.

I will keep a tally of the bank balance, though not of the bills.

The purpose of this diary is to focus on what I want so let's go to the land of imagination and look into my future. We will go ten years ahead.

In ten years.........

I have created a growing community. I have set up foundations and am helping to teach communities and cultures such as the Balinese how to grow organic food and how to be self-sufficient.

I have investment properties. These are my retirement funds.

I own a couple in Australia and a couple overseas. Whether I am buying or leasing them is irrelevant as it does not really matter. What is important is that I love my lifestyle and I love being able to travel. I have writing retreats in the mountains and by the beach.

My partner has his workshop and his boy's toys. I have my

studio, nature retreats and my toys. We get plenty of balance with our family life, plus we travel and spend time overseas.

The travelling pace is easy with lots of time in warm tropical climates. I love eating tropical fruits and I have plenty of them to eat. Pineapples, mangos, pawpaw, coconuts, mangosteen and other fresh organic yummy fruits at my fingertips.

I love being in the warm. I love being by the beach and I love the clean beautiful water.

My expert team are at home base and they are running everything.

Everything I need is in place.

I love and appreciate my team as they are as committed to the cause as I am. We have connected so many families and communities together. We have helped so many people that there are too many to count, it is so much more than I could ever have imagined. There are so many emails and letters each day that one person is employed just to sort it all. I love hearing all the great stories from people about how their lives have been transformed after they have been connected to my talks, teachings and books.

I see the web of my organisation spreading out.

My pace of life is easy and relaxed. My children come and stay with me often and they bring all the grandchildren. I love being a grannie. Money is no problem for me or them. I love my grandchildren and they have a great time staying with me. We have a fabulous time and life is great. Life is good and I feel blessed and appreciative.

I feel relaxed and free. It is a blessed feeling of being grateful for all the lives I have helped change and the differences I have made by sharing my gifts.

I will meditate on this feeling and bring this energy into my life today, right now.

As I bring this energy in, I appreciate having helped so many people and changing so many lives.

I feel this coming into my reality. I feel my body release and relax. I have a deeper sense of relaxation and calm.

That sounds like a great theme for a frustrated business woman today.

I feel all the blessings from all the lives that I have helped. I feel the gratitude from these people. I feel it touch my heart as I become open and aware of their appreciation.

I ask source, the universe, God, whatever you want to call it, it does not matter, to allow me to be a magnet for those wanting to feel blessed, free and happy.

I am ready and open for this in my life right now.

I know I am a writer, teacher, evangelist and cultural integrator primarily.

I bring people together and educate them. I bring families together. This is my gift and I am grateful for these gifts.

I will sit with that and touch base later.

Have a good day. I am sure I will now!!

Where will your life be in 10 years?

Day 3

Morning all.

Another cold and chilly Melbourne morning.

Money check in - I have $83 to spend - $15.88 bill so $67. I have $150 in my Paypal account.

Yesterday I was learning how to put together a well-manicured presentation. It was good.

I found the concepts that I learned very valuable as I can use these concepts in many areas of my life. I look forward to applying what I have learnt.

I am going to get a title today for the work that I do. I was thinking about the title 'From Fucked to Freedom.' A little blunt I know, though I am a real and raw person who loves to say it as it is.

My work is a compilation of all my learnings over the years.

It is composed of all the many, many tools, training, education and practices that I have learnt, experienced and accumulated. It is these tools that I use to help guide others to emotional and mental freedom as well as opening the doors to spiritual awakening.

So today is the day for moulding and sculpturing this information into a form that I can share with others.

The workshop I have been attending finishes at 7.30-8pm. They are long days.

This is why I did not write any more yesterday. I went to a friend's house instead and I caught up with all the gossip. It was nice to have some girlie time, it is important to us women to go bla bla bla and to debrief.

It's cold here and I am ready for a shower and everyone is asleep, so I am writing and meditating.

So let's do some forward business projection.

Let's put something into my future vortex or future space.

I would like to know, explore and face what financial freedom looks like to me.

I am great at what I do, I have amazing talents and skills, I present well, I am educated and a great motivational speaker and teacher. I am not sure if you have heard all this before.

I do ask myself what is the end result of doing this stuff?

What does it mean and what will it bring me?

What is it that I want?

Some financial freedom would be great. I will explore what that means to me.

Financial Freedom means to me….

- Buying organic food when I want. Having the freedom to go where I want to buy organic food because I want high quality, nutrient rich, vital foods. I to be able to eat whatever I choose and in the volumes that I want. My fridge is full of high quality organic food for my family. I even gift my family organic hampers of treats that they love. Yum.

- I have the freedom to go away when I want, in fact if I have a few days free I can shoot over to places like Bali, Vanuatu or Thailand to relax and write there for a while. I can shoot off for a weekend away when and where I choose because finding and paying for accommodation is easy.

- I eat when I want and I can go where I want, when I want in whatever mode I want. In fact on my many flights I travel business class because I like to have a comfortable sleep on the way and that is priceless to me.

- I wear remarkable and fabulous clothes and I look and feel great. Everything that I own or buy supports sustainable industries and organic growers.
- I have a cleaner and a gardener because I want to free up my time to do other things and cleaning is something I am happy to share with others. This leads me to do more things that I like to do. Creative and fun things with my valuable time.
- I have my virtual assistant and I have my marketing team. They help me with all the time consuming little jobs that I do not like to do. This is great as this frees up more time for me to be pursuing the things that I love to do.
- My staff help by doing buffer posts, answering emails, answering calls, doing sales calls, organising advertising campaigns, getting bums on seats, organising catering, plus other jobs. I also have two people who run my herb business. They order, pack and post for me, as well as updating social media and websites. This makes life easy for me, which is good.
- All my team are there for me and are willing to do what is required to keep the wheels of progress moving forward. And so it is. This sounds simple and yet it is easily achievable.
- The feeling component of this is because I like to feel special and I like to feel valued. I like to feel free. I like adventure. I like to feel happy. I like to feel blessed. I like to feel alive. I like to see new spaces and places. I like to be in joy.

I am on the journey of creating what I want and it is important to know the reasons why I want it. This is a great way to manifest.

When we use affirmations and say 'universe give me this and this.' it will not work if there is no feeling component involved. I know from personal experience. I have used unsuccessful affirmations for years and years.

I now know affirmations have to be a feeling thing.

Be IN it, feel yourself in your daydreams.

Live it. Add because to all your desires.

Think, want, feel.

I think this is a great idea. I love my little manifestation dream I had right there, it felt so good. I am open for this to come to fruition and I feel good things are coming my way. Onwards and upwards.

12.59 P.M.

Time for a money check - Money still the same

I am feeling a bit bla right now and the 'What's the use?' feeling is back.

It could have been the glass of wine that I had for breakfast. I am sure that did not help.

I am running one of my workshops at the weekend and I have few people booked in. It seems so hard getting bums on seats. It does not really matter what it is, workshops, seminars or courses. I seem to have problems getting numbers up for attendance.

I have been doing this and that. Then this and that and nothing seems to help. I have worked so hard and I have studied so much over the last two years. I would have though all this knowledge I have learnt would have paid off by now.

I feel quite despondent about my home situation. It is quite easy to get despondent when I keep working hard. I am doing, sorting and learning so much new stuff. Learning programs, new software, new processes that it goes on and on. I know have to get my positioning right, which is what needs to happen.

Because of this I am writing about this and this is part of what this diary is all about. It's creating a friend for me. Someone I can whinge to, share with and to debrief with and it helps to get it out of my system.

I will choose to explore where this journal will take me.

I have worked so hard all my life for so little reward. Long hours and physically hard and now I am realising that it is not about working hard, it is about working wise.

What is this feeling that I have?

Despondency. I choose to release that. I will let go of the 'what's the use?' feeling. How I am going to do this is to write myself 100 lines.

This makes a big difference for me and will help as I am rewiring my brain.

I will do that now.

1. I run a successful business
2. I run a successful business
3. I run a successful business
4. I run a successful business
5. I run a successful business
6. I run a successful business
7. I run a successful business
8. I run a successful business
9. I run a successful business
10. I run a successful business
11. I run a successful business
12. I run a successful business
13. I run a successful business
14. I run a successful business
15. I run a successful business
16. I run a successful business
17. I run a successful business
18. I run a successful business
19. I run a successful business
20. I run a successful business

21. I run a successful business
22. I run a successful business
23. I run a successful business
24. I run a successful business
25. I run a successful business
26. I run a successful business
27. I run a successful business
28. I run a successful business
29. I run a successful business
30. I run a successful business
31. I run a successful business
32. I run a successful business
33. I run a successful business
34. I run a successful business
35. I run a successful business
36. I run a successful business
37. I run a successful business
38. I run a successful business
39. I run a successful business
40. I run a successful business
41. I run a successful business
42. I run a successful business
43. I run a successful business
44. I run a successful business
45. I run a successful business
46. I run a successful business
47. I run a successful business
48. I run a successful business
49. I run a successful business
50. I run a successful business
51. I run a successful business
52. I run a successful business
53. I run a successful business
54. I run a successful business

55. I run a successful business
56. I run a successful business
57. I run a successful business
58. I run a successful business
59. I run a successful business
60. I run a successful business
61. I run a successful business
62. I run a successful business
63. I run a successful business
64. I run a successful business
65. I run a successful business
66. I run a successful business
67. I run a successful business
68. I run a successful business
69. I run a successful business
70. I run a successful business
71. I run a successful business
72. I run a successful business
73. I run a successful business
74. I run a successful business
75. I run a successful business
76. I run a successful business
77. I run a successful business
78. I run a successful business
79. I run a successful business
80. I run a successful business
81. I run a successful business
82. I run a successful business
83. I run a successful business
84. I run a successful business
85. I run a successful business
86. I run a successful business
87. I run a successful business
88. I run a successful business

89. I run a successful business
90. I run a successful business
91. I run a successful business
92. I run a successful business
93. I run a successful business
94. I run a successful business
95. I run a successful business
96. I run a successful business
97. I run a successful business
98. I run a successful business
99. I run a successful business
100. I run a successful business

Did you read it 100 times??

8.35 P.M.

Money check in - I have $61 in my account and a $63 herb order came in.

My partner gave me $150, I spent $51 on shopping.

Today has been a day of catching up, after being away for three days.

I like to do my positive affirmations out loud. I choose to say or write them in twenties or one hundred lots at one go. Today I did this twice, so that is two lots of one hundred.

You got a taste of that in my last entry.

It is far more powerful to write these in the present tense such saying 'I am' statements, though they can be spoken. The trick to doing these spoken is to speak it fast because the repetition rewires the brain and the myelin sheath.

I said the statement "I value myself and I give value."

Then I said "People want to give me money" also 100 times.

It does not take very long to do this and I like to when I am walking the dogs early in the morning. I like to use this time to do positive self-talk or to affirm myself.

I did earn some money today, I was also given some money and I posted some products. This is more business than the last week or so. My partner gave me some money as he has gone away and he knows things are tight for me right now. That was very kind of him and I appreciate him doing that.

Maybe I could do some other affirmations? Saying things like "Money is coming in from clients". That could be considered for tomorrow.

Today I got creative.

I got six huge pieces of card and I wrote up my business journey. I wrote my plans, my visions and my future outlook.

It was huge awareness for me and was extremely insightful.

These sheets explored,

1. Getting started
2. My transformational journey
3. The big picture of what I am doing
4. Road blocks that get in my way
5. Launching what I do
6. My seed sheet

It has been extremely helpful as I have colour coded them.

Green means I am on track and it has happened or is sorted. Orange means it is in the process and there is still more to go. Red means I have a block there business and it is not moving at all.

I realised that my message to the public and to myself is not clear and I want to get some clarity with that. So I am going to do a seed sheet about this. A seed sheet is a way of exploring and unpacking what it is I want to share with my tribe.

I feel less frustrated now I have done these charts and have seen that I have done a lot of foundational preparation. It is important to get my message and positioning right, otherwise how will people out there know what I am sharing?

I have thought of using the term CEE Me ™.

This is for Connecting, Earthing and Educating.

These three words resonate very strongly with me. They would be the areas I would want to educate and guide people. I believe in helping people to become self-sustaining and for them to be driving and guiding their own life.

Connecting is about connecting to your body, mind, spirit, and family. Once you are connected, or tuned in, turned in and tapped on then it is possible to create from that space.

Earth is about earthing and grounding yourself, respecting the earth and feeling alive and energised.

Educate is about empowering yourself and others with knowledge. So let's unpack and explore these.

Stories are vital with any message and I have lots of stories and experiences about connecting to others as well as connecting to my body. I also know the power of presence and how powerful it is to be present and how to use it.

I was president of the local BNI network group and I learnt about the power of connection. I also understand the power of being present in your body. How can we connect to others if we are not connecting to ourselves?

Connection can be likened to a tree connecting its roots into the ground which is keeping it secure and strong. This starts to touch on the word earthing, as this is what grounding is about. I have proved the power of this and I understand the power of presence and knowing how empowering embodiment is.

The processes of connection can be found by doing what I call dropping in or tuning yourself inwards. Once you can be aware of what being present is and can learn whether or not you are in your body, then following on from this it is common practice to teach people how to create your boundaries and contain your own energy in them.

I have methods and processes have been learnt, created or I have downloaded in dreams and meditations around these practises. This is what I love to teach.

This is an example of unpacking the word connection. I am going to do the same with the words earth and educate, right now.

Day 4

Money Check - Not sure of my bank balance, I spent 14.95 and $59

It's the afternoon and I am off teaching.

I pulled the pin on my workshop at the weekend, it was not worth it. Too much stress and I do not need it.

I had two or maybe three people who wanted to come and they wanted to be on a payment plan and that is not going to work for me as it would cost me for the venue, food, staff and it would all be coming out of my pocket. This is not divine timing.

The more I keep affirming my value the more I am becoming intolerant of doing things for others and the more I am putting myself first.

This is with my customers and also in my relationships with others. I do not need to muck around with payment plans and chasing people for money. I am ready to keep moving forward and to be honouring myself.

I am going to do a five minute manifestation.

I was chatting with a friend and saying "Let's go move to Vanuatu." So let's go to make believe.

I am overseas and I am living overseas.

For how long, it does not matter. One month, one year, the time frame is irrelevant, what matters is the fact that I am there.

I love my lifestyle, finally it is warm, I feel warm, inspired and I create.

I am surrounded by nature, green colours, birds, dogs and animals. They are all coming in and out of where I live and they are hanging around to share their love. I sit and watch the joy on their faces.

This morning as I was walking the dogs someone said "Look at your happy friends." And he was right. They are all my happy friends and they are so easy to please. I am living and enjoying with my animal friends in Vanuatu.

I do not have any responsibilities. I can do whatever, whenever. I am not tied to a schedule. I have my own personal routine.

I get up. I chat to the animals. I welcome the love and embrace Mother Nature. I go for a walk or a swim, meditate, take in Mother Nature and I am present in all that.

I have time in my life to practise presence.

After that I go off to eat and I chat with my tribe and answer any questions that they may have. I attend to my group or team and spend an hour or so attending to business. I check in with my virtual assistant (VA) and with my personal assistant (PA). It's all good and I have a great team doing their thing and they love it too.

I go and have lunch and decide how I am going to spend my afternoon. My partner is away so I have the space and time. I decide to do something creative and to paint. I go to my studio to start painting.

I create something beautiful. I see the colours, the teals, blues, greens, oranges and yellow. It's a colourful creation. Its great having a space where I can leave it up and pick it up again when I choose. There is no need to pack anything away. This place is a great studio.

The biggest thing about this creation is the time factor. I do not need to look at the clock, I am in joy time.

There are no deadlines. I am here and I have set up my passive incomes and made all the things in my life automated. All the systems, models and templates have been put in place. I have done the hard yards and now I reap the benefits.

As I paint I feel the inspiration and creative energy coming in. I have a great idea and I pick up the pen and paper and I write it down. I love the feeling of having the inspiration just come. I do not have to chase anything. Things come to me now. It just flows and I feel it flowing through me. It feels great this feeling of divine flow, I love it.

It's a lovely cool evening and I sit and watch the sunset over the trees and the water. A cat comes and shares some love with me, we share some joy together as the sunsets over the trees and the water.

What a great relaxing and joyous day. I appreciate these days as it took a while to change my mindset and to stop pushing and start receiving.

I slowly let the joy seep into my soul. I own it and it feels good.

That was my manifestation vision.

Let's get on with business.

I am unpacking the three words, connect, earth and educate. This means I will see my customers, see what they want, see their language and their lifestyle, know what their hesitations are and then I will see what benefits they will have by working with me.

I will unpack all three words and see if I will be able them all today.

I am doing my business unpacking and exploration in another book, though if I have any inspiration I will share them here.

So later Vanuatu trippers.

6.45 P.M.

Back again and I am just touching base.

I was teaching for the first time in seven years and I loved it. It was great.

I spent time writing and exploring the word 'connect.' I found and unpacked some interesting stuff which was good, so I will share some info about it here.

My feet hurt by the way. I am back in the high heels and I have to get used to wearing them again.

I became aware that it is time to start sharing my expertise.

I was writing about my avatar's (perfect customer) hesitations.

I discovered that they want to be heard and they want a deeper connection with themselves and their partners. An awakening that so many people 'suffer in silence.' I think that is good wording to use.

I then listed the benefits of working with them that was great. I realised that I have a lot more to offer than I give myself credit for.

It was a good job done. I have plenty of focus now.

I will go home and add to my huge charts on the wall and make some new large mind map pictures. I think I will take photos of them. That sounds like a plan.

It is important to know what my marketing message is.

From there it is the case of spending thousands of hours repeating the same formula over and over again, using my terminology, sharing my vision and getting my words out there. Over time people will understand my message.

It feels good to know my direction that I want to relay to the world.

I was productive and motivated today.

I also rang many old clients to get an understanding of their terminology and the words that they use when they describe me, the work I do with them, how working with me has benefited them and what do they like about what I do. It was a great exercise and was great for boosting morale.

It is important for me to know what the word on the street is, so to speak.

It is these very phrases that I can use. Someone said 'You helped stopping me from flipping my shit.' Now I could not have made that up myself. It is a great line. Thanks guys.

Once I understand the terminology of my tribe and words or

phrases that they use, then I have to know what strategies I will use to get them out there.

I like networking, I love public speaking and I am good at it, I love doing video vlogs and educational things like webinars.

Maybe I can do more online courses?

Then I have to entice people in with freebies. Mmm, I will have to give that some thought. These are the marketing drivers that will bring in the emails and phone numbers.

Maybe a video series is a good idea I think.

Maybe I can do some downloadable PDF's and cheat sheets, or even some free mini courses. I do have to drive the leads to where I want them to be.

Maybe I have too many choices and it can spread me thin? I have be advised to do three things and aim to do them well. Though sounds like sound advice.

So I will recap – what are my marketing strategies that I like?

- Public speaking has to be number one, I love it
- You Tube videos, I enjoy them too
- Blogs, I know they have to be regular
- Social media – now that can be distracting
- Doing some alliances or joint ventures could be a possibility
- Giving away some freebies

My marketing drivers then will be

- Speaking again, especially for other people
- Webinars
- Workshops
- My video series. This could be 144 topics. I like this number.
- Cheat sheets and downloadable courses or info
- My newsletter

That looks like a good start to me.

I have a client who booked in on Saturday.

I believe the business energy is starting to shift already.

That's $100 and then someone asked me to do a cleaning and repair job for them, so that is more bills that can get paid.

It's imperative that I advertise my services tomorrow.

It's all very well being the best kept secret, though it is important to let others know what I do. I want to start doing my amazing healing schedule tonight and to get that started.

I need to find a pencil for that. I wish I could find my pencil case. Actually I think I know where it is. I think it is in the back of the car. I will check it out.

Write or right! I will keep on listing and exploring and unpacking what it means and what my message and journey means.

Day 5

Money check - Bank balance is about $60 in there

I have to pay a guy back for the deposit for the workshop that I cancelled. That is $300, plus I have a zoom bill that just came out, without letting me know.

I also need to buy milk and feed the kids and I feel like shit today.

I feel like a failure. I have just been cleaning a friend's house because she is away and her place has been broken into by a psycho ex-partner. There was glass everywhere and he went through all her personal items including her underwear. She is away and does not want to come back to that mess. I do not blame her. I was happy to help her out. I would like it if someone did the same for me.

Anyway it gives me some money. While I was cleaning I am thinking this is crap. All these qualifications and expertise and I am cleaning a house. I keep getting paid small amounts for shit work when I would rather be paid large amounts for minimal work. I am not happy about it and I am feeling quite despondent.

I am just going to sit with my emotional pain.

I feel overwhelmed with financial pressure and I had a little cry.

I feel fear and I know my light will not shine as long as I feel fear and doubt.

It is time to change this and turn this around.

It's time for money to start coming in. It's time to start allowing great things to come in and for myself to be open to this healing and abundant presence.

It is time to let the fear go. I feel crushed about money. I have let it crush me for a lot of my life.

Universe please help me to unfurl and release this crushed feeling. I want to shine and not feel crushed. I want to be free. I want my light to shine for others to see it shine. I want to be a guide and inspiration to others.

It is good for me to focus on what I want, otherwise I can get lost in feeling shit.

I think I will shower, go quote this job and then go from there.

I have a friend who is a marketing lady coming over. It seems like it is all sort of crumbling around me today, so I will see how it goes.

Shower, clean, fill the hunger in my belly and eat.

9.15 P.M.

I was answering some questions that I came across and I thought it would be a good place to do it here.

1. What do I want to be known for? – I want to be known for 'changing people's lives.' Having a mine of knowledge, giving really good information and support to others. She knows her stuff and she runs Earth Church.
2. What is my reason for living? – My reason for living is to be a teacher, a spiritual educator that awakens others and helps them to shine their light. This is my destiny and is my calling. I love to feel the love coming through my body and my being.

3. What is my vision? – My vision is to change the consciousness of the planet by realigning and connection.

4. What are my values? – I live for being real, for letting it out, for finding easy solutions, for honouring the earth and ourselves.

5. What do you have courage for? – I have courage to help people to connect to themselves and to others.

6. Who are my heroes? – Ester Hicks, Phillip Day, Don Tolman

7. What is my expertise? – Teaching, public speaking, writing, content, organisation, leadership.

8. What is my profession? – Teaching, facilitating, author.

9. What are my greatest accomplishments? – Being published, establishing an organic farm, healing events, running herb growing networks, writing courses, being student, raising my family.

10. When I die I will be remembered for? – Louise was a dedicated and passionate teacher and spiritual educator who dedicated her life to healing and supporting others to find their freedom in all aspects of their lives. We have all seen this ripple spread as her love revolution shed its light upon the world.

Some great questions hey?
Feel free to add your own answers.

Day 6

Money Check - I have another $160 in the bank as I got paid for cleaning.

Some random money came out of my bank account for something I had not counted on. I hate it when unexpected money just comes out my account. I think it is common courtesy to inform you first before taking money out.

I am feeling a little more hopeful today and far better than I was feeling yesterday. I still keep on keeping on.

I have a mission today, to advertise myself and maybe do it continually and even consistently. That would be a good idea.

I have courses, products and other stuff I offer, so I have to 'get with the program.'

I started doing feminine presence mediation again today. I did it yesterday and today and both days made me cry, which is a good thing. I am letting go.

I was thinking that being more disciplined with my self-care routine would be a great idea. My self-care routine looks like this

- Meditation
- Promote myself

- Attend to my social media group
- Find more social media friends

This would give me a daily routine or ritual to sort out.

I could call it my 'routual', he he, I love making up words.

This will help me to build my tribe and my following. This is Plan A.

I could add these things to my To Do list.

Each week I write a To Do list, I am very organised like that. I usually do it on a Sunday night or Monday morning. It gives me focus and direction for the week and I like to be organised.

I can have between eight to twenty things on my To Do list each week and if I do not get them done, they get carried over to the following week. Successful people write lists and it works for me.

This is what my list is starting to look like for the week

- Doing livestreams
- Webinars
- Sales calls
- Speaking requests
- Client calls
- Newsletter emails
- Freebie posts

This looks good, as long as I do not extend myself too far.

If I plot and record my weekly activity of doing this I can see where my weakest link is.

It is time for change. I want to bring in some abundant energy. Energy in, equals energy out.

Maybe it is worth considering and even thinking about what it feels like when I help someone and they hand me money.

I feel appreciated, I feel happy, I feel loved, I feel (words are coming to my head saying "You must do this, you must do this,").

I know where those words come from, though I know they are not serving me.

Ok let me release some of that and write about some of these Must Do's.

I let go of some unwanted energy and after doing that awareness comes.

It was a feeling about control, about feeling that 'I have to do this' and 'I have to do that.' I know how important it is to have a plan and to follow it. I have committed to changing the way I do business and that is why I signed up for Business Mastery training because I believed in myself enough to do it. Now I am making changes for me.

Maybe I can make a contract with myself and I can sign up for that. That would make sense. That would show my level of commitment.

I know I am going in circles. I like systematics, so I will create a system and a way of making things easier and more automated for me.

I am feeling quite pumped now so I am going to advertise my services. It is always a good idea to write stuff or make promotional posts when feel I positive and pumped. Ok, off to do it, time is ticking on.

Day 7

Money check - $100 from a client came in.

I have had two clients book in over the next 24 hour period. Woo Hoo.

Things are starting to change. That is the aim of this diary. I can feel the energy shift already.

I had all intentions of writing yesterday afternoon, though I got busy. If you do not hear from me then it is quiet time or I am busy. So that is a good thing.

I did a free talk yesterday evening and one client booked in for next Monday and possibly another one coming. I also manifested some email addresses, so the talk worked well.

I spoke with the guy that I did my speaking workshop with last week and he came up with a great marketing message. I like it.

I did two picture templates this morning to use on social media which rock. They look good.

I also got inspiration about creating some short courses on detoxing, so I will start that soon. Inspiration is flowing in today and it feels great.

I did a plan to help me with what I am doing. I advertised myself yesterday and will do the same today, though in the afternoon. I got another client who also booked in, so that is good too.

I wrote two sales funnels in the afternoon, a money cheat sheet called 'Ten Money Making Steps', of which my sixteen year old son edited for me. He is studying English literature and his grammatical knowledge is priceless.

We teach best what we most need to know.

So things are starting to move now. I have my message which is great and I will sit with that, as I want that to feel right. I can change some of my red and orange stickers to green ones, according to my traffic light system on my business overview charts.

My clearer message is about the 'Higher Laws.' The higher laws are like living with the natural laws of the universe. An example would be something like, we can not unlearn something once we know it. I will work out the rest.

I will do a livestream about it that and why it is important.

I said on my 'To Do' list that I was going to do two livestreams a week. I might record a zoom message as well. I hope that that is not over extending myself as I do have a habit of doing that. I will try it out and see how it goes.

My plan gives me an idea of what I am to target each week and it includes

- Two livestreams
- Ten potential sales calls
- Write a newsletter
- Go to my networking group
- Do twenty Facebook posts over my many pages

I am also must be spending more conscious time connecting in. I did the feminine presence meditation yesterday and that is two days in a row. That works for me, which is great. It is helping me to feel more aligned, centred, present, and empowered and they have to be a good thing. We can all benefit from that.

I will write some manifestation words of what I want. If I do this it will pump me up for my livestream.

I am feeling the good feeling.

I want freedom, happiness, joy, excitement, adventure, laughter, abundance, choice, easy, may options, exploration, friskiness, and appreciation.

I will finish by saying 'Thank You Universe' for the clients that have booked in within the last twenty four hours.

I appreciate you answering my call and bringing people to me. I know I am a great and amazing healer and I have lots of expertise to offer. I have helped two people out of wheel chairs and I do not acknowledge that about myself enough.

Things are always working out for me.

1.45 P.M.

Money check - I checked my bank and I have $213, woo hoo.

Another client booked in. I really feel that things are starting to move for me. Maybe this diary might work after all. I can go and buy a pencil case now, yee har. I even bought some doggy treats. Things are looking up and it is good for me to acknowledge that.

So let's manifest and ride the feel good wave.

Part of the aim of this diary is to write or spend thirty minutes a day focusing on what I want, rather than keep focusing on being broke. So here goes.

How will my business give me money?
What are the ways that money can come to me?

I can put up eight courses in the future, three of which be freebies.

I can earn money from my online courses, this is great passive income.

Hang on a minute …. It is important to talk about this in the present NOW tense for this to work so I will correct myself.

I have lots of online courses to sell.

I give away free courses to those who are keen to learn more or who want to be introduced to my work.

I love earning passive income from my online courses and teachings.

I have income coming in from clients.

I know my message and I help people to find the clarity and answers that they want in their lives, either in a one to one or a group setting.

I help people to learn about the benefits and the pitfalls of detoxing. I offer help, information, support, education, and even the space to come and detox with me. People want to have clarity on their health and wellbeing.

People want to have answers that will really work.

People see me as the expert that I am. People want to buy my books, love my alkaline water machines, want my herbs, want my teas, and my superherb products.

People value one on one time with me.

People want to do my seminars, my workshops and my retreats. They want to be a part of the ongoing services that I have.

People pay to hear me speak. They want to be a part of the many avenues and journeys that I have.

People grow and learn with me.

People want training in my processes, they want to teach and share processes with others.

People come and want anything that I have to offer because my message is clear.

People want to step into 'The Higher Laws.'

People want to feel aligned and want healing. This deepens their connection and I see this process for them to grow and flourish.

The healing that occurs is one thing and this leads onto other services that I have to offer.

My connection with my customers and clients increases. Our healings strengthen our earth connections and allows us to step into our true sovereignty. We all educate ourselves to deepen the knowledge, wisdom and connection that we have.

We earth ourselves to increase healing and grounding. This strengthens our connection and helps us to become more empowered.

My key words are linked and they easily work together, for the benefit of each other.

Healing to connection, to earthing to awakening to education to sovereignty.

And so on, I will now meditate on this intertwining.

I do not think I will get to chat later as I am going to keep writing this detox process. I feel quite rushed and I want to ground my alignment and the good feeling that I have right now.

I AM a successful business woman,

I AM a successful business woman.

Day 8

Money Check - Bank balance is $160, plus $83. Internet bill is due end of month.

I was just making anagram from the first letter of key words I like.

C, H, E, A, S, E was the closest I came to making a word. It was a bit of silly fun. You might come up with something better.

It's a cold and windy day here, looks like there will be a biting wind out there.

Dark and cold, it makes me think and dream of warm beaches.

I have a client at 11.30, Yipee. That's great, my manifesting is creating stuff and I am very pleased about that.

Last night I ended up finishing my charts and getting them up on the wall. I only have the unpacking of the seed sheets left to go. This is all about my exploring my own intellectual property. It is like I do not have to be like anyone else anymore. I do not have to compare or follow the format of anyone else. I can just be me and do my thing. It is me following and stepping into my own genius and sharing the unique gifts that I have.

This is like a relief because I do find I compare myself to others. I look at what others are doing and I say 'I can do that.' The reality I see now is for me to do what I am best at.

What confuses me is that I can do sooo much and have done so much that I do not know what that 'thing' is. This is why I call myself an infopreneur rather than an entrepreneur. I said I like making up words.

I will do some painting today which will a good idea. I would like to do some gardening though it looks COLD!

It's time for some future lifestyle manifestations.

Knowing my intellectual property and my message is about sharing 'The Higher Laws.'

These are laws that we have that we live by. They are natural laws we are best abiding by. They are important. They are sort of like karma. So you sow, so you will reap.

10.40 A.M.

I got distracted by pruning fruit trees, where was I?

I was manifesting my future, OK how does that look? ....

It is my message sharing what The Higher Laws are all about. I will write about this to manifest and put energy out into the universe about it.

I could create a pod cast, this feels like a great idea.

Manifestation must be present tense, remember?

I pick a weekly discussion or topic about what I am learning about. It is about the knowledge that is coming through. Yesterday while doing the feminie presence meditation I saw the geometry shapes for the male and the female. I also saw where the motion is and where the direction of the energy flows for both genders.

I have my podcast and I am making a weekly recording for about ten to fifteen minutes. This starts to get a following and people start to listen.

I have twelve times twelve topics of information that I will present and unpack as my intellectual property (IP). This means that I have 144 topics. These topics can go on and on. After 144 weeks I will be able to replicate them or chose something new.

I pod cast, email, livestream, and add to my newsletter and my FB groups.

I use my language that will come out with the wisdom and knowledge that I share to my tribe that till now has been packed up. Now it will be seeded out into the community.

The tribe loves that and the repetition starts to go out far and wide, so much so that people want to learn more. They want to get to know and learn more about what I have to share. They want to do my courses and attend my events. They are hungry for more. They are willing to pay for more.

So much so I see myself hiring staff. My personal assistant is the first of many. It does not take long and soon I have three staff.

My first staff member is still doing the funnels and marketing. My virtual assistant (VA) is still doing the management of the FB pages.

As things start to get busier I realise that I need a personal assistant. This is someone to help me type up content, organize marketing and make phone calls. My assistant has the gift of mercy and hospitality which lets them give our clientele the personal touch that they deserve to have, want and need.

They have great ideas and they all love the work that they do. The tribe love the personal touch.

My team loves to give great value as they know the power of gifting and giving and so the ripple spreads out to the world. We all acknowledge that what we are doing is helping to life the vibration of humanity and this is a great cycle of events.

I continue to unpack and seed the 144 items that I have and so it goes on and on. This gives me limitless content. After all I am the content queen.

This is great, my topics begin and they just keep rolling of the tongue. This is a weekly process of unpacking and this could easily take two years.

I AM the content queen afterall!

The process is the process of growth. I let the first dozen begin and momentum flows from there. One item moves gracefully into another.

This week or starting Monday will be the first topic and this is the topic Connect. I will record information about connecting and I will define my message.

I contact other podcasters and I connect with them.

I know people make wiser choices when they become informed and educated. I can email it, blog it, vlog it, I just love to share my knowledge. This is my subject and it helps to take people to where they want to go. This is why education is one of my three core topics. This is the place to start and to let it evolve.

We connect to ourselves and then we can connect to the light, connect to our bodies, connect to our food, connect to our families, and community.

I will let my radiance shine.

I reread that and I hope it makes sense.

I think I am excited and something new is going to start.

5.05 P.M.

It has been a good day of doing household chores.

I have been painting and putting together some online detox course info, one of which is eighty four pages.

It is good. I am getting my three day course together, so preparing, preparing.

There is much preparing to do.

The cats on me now!

It's so cold out here in my living room. It's very cold and I am not a lover of winter months, the dark, the biting wind and the chilly mornings.

I am distracted now, dinner, chickens, making salad, and getting daily chores done. It is that busy time of night with animals and children to feed and sort out.

Okay, because I have so much to do I want to talk about organisational skills.

It is important for me to be mindful of how I spend my time.

I am an organised person and can be anally so. I hate being late and rushing things at the very last minute.

The only thing I never usually prepare for is when I do public speaking gigs. I always know my topic, though when I am up there I just channel and let inspiration come through. Some of the best talks I have ever given are when I do not remember what I was talking about. It is like I just channel the teachings. People have come up to me afterwards and said it was amazing and life changing.

I did this exercise once that is called a RAC. Record, analyse and change.

I logged my daily activities in ten minute slots for about four days. I did not need to do any longer because four days was enough for me to know what my time wasters were.

Talking on the phone was number one. Spending time on social media was number two.

Then the third was pottering around, pretending I was house cleaning, moving shit about and stuff like that. I knew I had to change things.

I limited my phone calls to ten minutes only, unless it was an out of business hours social call. I stopped the Facebook time wasting and I limited my time on there from 9 a.m. to 9.30 a.m. This meant I only check in once a day. Now that worked.

From here I was able to schedule my time into thirty minute slots. This meant I was then not working until 9 p.m. at night. Because of this my time has become more focused and organised.

It can be a problem when one works from home and for one's self.

Now this might sound anal to many, though when you work for yourself, you can either pretend that you are running a hobby business and I can be living like I have been or I can start to get serious about what and where I am going. It is distractions and time wasting that stops me from moving forward.

A good question all you self-employed people can ask yourself is, "What type of employee would I be to someone else?" Answer that and that will tell you what kind of employee you are to yourself.

Right then, off to do the next thing now.

I am writing systems and processes, it would be good to stop and turn it off.

Running a business is an ongoing thing.

Plan, plan, plan, plan. Slowly, slowly moving forward.

It would be good to meditate now and ground my flow feeling once again.

Day 9

I have been meditating today. It was good. I was visualising seeing my radiance shining out to the world. I grounded myself and then put myself in my body. From there I was shining my light (change of pen) out to the world for all to see.

I could see my message. 'The Higher Laws' and I saw it earthing into the ground.

Once earthed in the ground I saw it put its roots into the earth, right down in to the crystalline bed at the centre of the earth. From the roots I could see the energy grow and grow up and start to create branches. The branches branched out, the earthing, the connecting, the educating, all branching out.

It was quite groovy and no mind altering substances were involved, it was a purely mediative state. My crazy days of that lifestyle are over.

My branches are coming out from these larger branches, moving out to smaller branches, all coming out and twisting out to smaller branches and twigs and finally to the leaves.

The leaves were like the tribe. They come and go, come and go. New ones, old ones, always moving on and on. It was a great visualisation.

As I was meditating I was also seeing my tribe, they are my people. Old souls, light workers empaths and those awakened to the light. I was letting them know that their shining light is enough. It's always enough just as it is.

It's good to know that we all have enough and that are enough. I like that.

I am going to pretend to play my violin for a bit.

Laters, I will keep visualising and I am off to my Earth Church. Chat later.

4.40 P.M.

I spent a lot of the day in the garden, which was great.

I was cleaning out more stuff that needed cleaning out and throwing away. There was some old metal stuff that was lying around the house and garden.

Then I went bush and attended my Earth Church. I experienced the same thing with seeing my roots going into the ground to ground my vision and my message.

What is Earth Church some of you might be saying?

Well here is the story and this is how it goes.

I found myself feeling like I wanted a spiritual mentor in my life. I looked around at some of the local churches and nothing was really calling me. It was not that I really wanted to celebrate He/She/Universe/God/Spirit, it was case of wanting somewhere to go and say a prayer, give an offering and ask for any help with issues that I had or questions I wanted answered.

So in the end I said bugger it, I will go and create my own church and this church will be a tree.

At that time I was feeling a little lost so I went and had a chat with a tree. I shared my problems, said a prayer, gave an offering of incense and then asked for some guidance.

I laid down on the ground and I looked up into the tree, I immediately saw inspiration and the advice that I was given seemed to be very useful. I like to go chat with a tree and attend my Earth Church as much as I can.

It has sort of become a thing and there has never been a time when I have not been guided to inspiration and had an answer to whatever it is that I am seeking. I now share my inspirations on my Instagram page.

That is what Earth Church is about.

I love it because Mother Nature gives me the answers that I am looking for, every time.

It feels good having some focus and direction after fourteen months of fumbling in the dark. Especially as I have been paying a juicy amount of money for the training I put my hand up for and I still have not been getting clearer on what it is that I am really doing when I grow up.

I decided I will start next week with my topic of the week and the topic of the week will be 'Connect.' I think I said that before.

I will explore this topic inside and out, I will unpack it and explore what it means to me. That sounds like a great plan, so let's do it now.

Why connect?

It is important to connect with other people as we are all important. We are social creatures and if we do not connect and bond together, then we can live a life of bondage. This bondage is about being closed down and feeling alone.

The only way that we really get to know each other is by sharing things about ourselves, how we feel, our dreams and passions and who we are. We do not get to really know others by what they do. We know others by who they are. This makes us closer to other human beings.

The question I then ask myself is how can we do this?

If we are connecting and understanding each other then we will relate to each other better. I see us getting along.

Share how things feel for you, share your dreams and share what lights you up. The most important thing is to open up your emotional body and to share your feelings.

This is a great expansion idea. I might do it in another book, haha.

For now I have decided that I will write all the ways and possibilities that I have to make money. I like this great manifestation process.

Who, What, when, why and how.

My list of how I can make money.

- Selling my herb teas
- Selling my herb powders
- People buying bulk herbs
- People buying bulk powders
- Shops wanting to stock herbs
- New business wanting herbs and herb products
- Getting paid for teaching
- People paying me to speak
- Selling my alkaline water machines
- People joining my lift off program
- People wanting consultations
- People wanting one to one time with me
- People wanting naturopathic consults
- People want spiritual healing
- People wanting counselling
- Couples wanting counselling
- People wanting hair analysis
- Doing handyman work, odd jobs
- Selling my paintings
- Selling crafts
- People wanting to do my seminars

- People wanting support with detoxing
- People signing up to one of my courses
- People signing up for three day detox
- Someone asking me to be a ghost writer
- My books getting published
- Someone pays for an article
- Someone pays me to write a course
- College offers me some tutoring and extra marketing
- I could get an inheritance
- My teas go on ebay
- Finding a diamond ring

Whenever I do this exercise I always start to think of other ways that I can start to bring money into my life. Once I start thinking of it, more ideas appear. I am open to these ideas coming to fruition. This is great. Bring it on.

I am open to receiving abundance in my life.

5.35 P.M.

Money Check - I have $260 in my bank, woo hoo

I have herb orders coming in which is great. This is really working!

I have been getting my VA to advertise on my Facebook page, the herb one. This is to increase traffic going to my online herb site. I am hoping this will increase business.

That's good. I have clients tonight and more tomorrow.

I actually got to order herbs via paypal, which was great. I look forward to the day when I can actually go shopping and I do not have to count my money as I put things in my basket.

I see that things are starting to move now. There is power on focusing on what I want rather than complaining about being poor.

So my aim this week is to share my message and I will start doing this by doing a livestream about it. I will also positively reinforce this here in this diary as that is what it is for. It is important for me to do my manifestations as if I was in it and as if it is happening in the here and now.

I have financial freedom to ......
I have financial freedom in my business and I do exactly what I want.

I am able to save and that feels great as I can work towards exciting adventures in my life. I take money from my bank whenever I want and I save easily.

I have the freedom to go away for writing retreats, weekends away as and when I choose. I do this because I know this is important to me. I go to a tropical island, to sit near the sand and beach and I feel the warm sun on my body. I love feeling the warmth on my body and to feel the cool clean sea as it washes away any troubles and cares I may have. It feels good to feel the sun on my body, I like it.

I love feeling the warmth as it opens me up. It opens up my creativity and my inspiration. This allows my genius to flow. Each day more and more of my inner genius continues to flow.

I allow my DNA to activate my genius. Each day more by more, the activation is happening. I know I am a divine being, I see and feel that.

What a nice manifestation, I could almost feel my body warming up.

I am mindful at the moment that one of my distractions is the fact that I am playing into other people's dramas.
Why do I do this?
Why is this important to us as humans to like drama?
I know I fall into distractions. I have not done my feminine meditation for the last two days and I notice the difference. I like

feeling centred and aligned. It is good for me and it is good for the all.

So I will write and explore any reasons why I get involved into other's dramas.

It makes me feel important because I know I am solution orientated and I can sort it out.

So am I getting involved for me or for them?

The drama comes and I get involved in it. It can come from the fact that these people do not want to sort things out themselves, they just like the drama and to drag other people into the story.

I learn to let other people's dramas go. Unless people are asking me for help I do not have time to listen to drama and stories. I am best sitting and waiting for them to come to me when they want help, otherwise I learn to turn my back on drama.

When I get lost in other's stuff I am taking myself away from my centre.

It is important for me to stay aligned and centred and to observe other people's games and drama's that they play. This is their story and their drama is nothing to do with me, it is my choice to get involved or not.

What would I rather be doing?

I am on my tropical island, I can see myself there.

I change the places that I go to. Vanuatu, Bali, Philippines, Samoa, and Fiji, even Thailand is fine. It is all fine. I choose to bring that into my life, right here and now.

I continually consciously turn on my radiance. I shine my light and I see my light radiating. Others will come. People will want to come to the radiance and the light. They will want to touch, taste, feel and see it. The light is in all that I do. It is in the words that I write, the herbs that I blend, the joy that I share, the mp3's that I record, the livestreams that I have, the joy that I share and the awakenings that I bring.

People want to share anything that I have created when my light shines. In fact it does not matter what it is, it is the just the fact that they want light in their lives to.

Whatever they buy or enlist to I teach people how to activate and shine their own light. My message will teach and show people how to maintain their own welling, health and space.

I will help to show and teach people how to heal themselves and bring their happiness from the inside out. After all it is an inside job. I feel the momentum building and I give gratitude for yesterday and gratitude for today.

In fact I have decided I am going to share as many daily appreciations as much as I can. I will start right now.

1. I appreciate spending time with my boys in the garden because it feels good
2. I appreciate taking my daughter to the bush and connecting with her and Mother Nature.
3. I appreciate the three herb orders I have received as I like sharing the love and I love the power of herbs.

Day 10

Money Check - Paid some bills, $180 to FB for add, $80 phone and website, still have internet to go. Have $250 left. Things are looking up!

I am on the train.

It has been a bit of a morning.

I chose to clean my house and listen to a man talk about forgiveness. It was very rewarding as the forgiveness that needs to happen is me forgiving myself first and foremost.

I see that now.

I see that people out there hurting themselves and others because they are disconnected from their true and higher selves. What a world would we live in if we could just learn to forgive? What a world would we live in if we all knew how important it is to connect to our higher and true selves? I think we would all be a lot happier and healthier.

I would want that for everyone out there.

I also want lunch. Ha ha. That is not funny, because I am hungry.

2 P.M.

I had some lunch, not the yummy lunch I would have preferred though that could be a story for another day or even for another diary.

I know that when I get stressed I can procrastinate. I do not like to do things like write newsletters or make phone calls when I feel blocked, feel shitty or when I am not in the flow.

Can I explain 'being in the flow'?

It is sort of the feel good feeling where I just feel good. All the traffic lights are on green and I just flow through life. That is a good way to describe it. I find myself meeting the right people at the right time, I ask for something and it turns up. Being in the flow is a feeling of being happy and wanting to share.

This is different from wanting to hide, though I do not want to focus on that energy too much. As I have said before, where the attention goes, the energy flows.

I will discuss my procrastination though because as I shine a light on it, it will cause it to change.

I procrastinate when I am stressed or overwhelmed. I let people distract me and I allow people to waste my time. I do not like 'naffing about' is one of my sayings. I can spend days and weeks avoiding, though in hindsight I usually avoid because I am not feeling good. I like to share when my love cup is filled inside.

I can naff about myself as well. I am very good at looking busy, when in reality I am not doing anything at all. I can be sitting on my computer, when really I am just surfing the web.

So what excuses do I often use myself?

I am too busy, I have too much to do, he or she made me do it, I feel like shit or what's the use?

I know these well and I do have the power and the tools to change all of these.

So let's do that.

I know the most important thing for me to do it to keep shining my light.

I am bringing the world the message of The Higher Laws. I am the goddess of The Higher Laws. This is my thing and my mission.

I am always studying and bringing more information in about it.

I believe now that is it time to start putting energy out. I have been studying far too long, wanting things to be right, feeling that if I just do this or if I just learn that, then I will be ready. I have covered my underlying insecurities by being an intellectual.

Well that is all bullshit and if I keep waiting for things to be perfect then I will never step out there. This is why I am doing my weekly 144 topics just to start getting out there. It does not matter if my videos are not perfect and it does not matter if I do not look quite right. What is important is that I am doing it and I am starting now.

Today I have been getting a presentation ready. It's time to get it started and to see it happening. I love public speaking.

I did a You Tube video about connection yesterday, plus I recorded an Mp3 about it.

Where do I put it? I do not know yet, I will just store them and save for another day.

What I do know is the unpacking process is just bringing me more and more content.

I want to take a photo of my business traffic light plans and then review it in a month and see where it is at.

Am I obsessed?

It might sound like it, though this diary is a space for me to talk about business. This is all about business and how I have been a wimpy, frustrated business woman and how I am working to turn this around.

You are my business colleague, my friend and I can tell you whatever I want and share whatever I want. This is one reason I am doing this is to be fully open and authentic here.

I am sure you know what it is like.

We say some things to some people and some different things to others. It is a relief and it is great to be able to tell all, that is the power of writing.

Writing helps to give me focus.

I have spent a long time focusing on what I want, on my business and on making plans for my future. I see myself as a conscious co-creator and part of this knows when and where I want or choose to go.

These are great things in my eyes.

I want clients, so I will use today's writings to manifest having clients and exploring what that means to me.

Why do I like having clients? …….

I love empowering people, I love helping them to get to the bottom of what is happening in their lives.

I like seeing them have solutions to the problems they come to me with. I know there is no problem that cannot be solved and I love to use simple ways to make their lives easier.

I like seeing people in their own power. I love seeing people filling their lives with love and happiness and to see that rippling out to their family and friends and into their community. I like seeing the relief that they have. I love seeing the light come on inside.

I like people knowing that they are their own doctor and that they have the power to take their life, their healing abilities and their health in their own hands. From there they can trust their own inner guidance and feelings about what feels right for them.

I see me passing on the light when in reality I am passing on the light. I am helping them to clear their own channel. I see my light being all they need to stimulate their life and their journey and to start the initiation process to change.

I see my radiance magnetised, I am a magnetised being who lets the light flow in and then sends it out to the world.

I ground that light and the light is love. It is love for sure.

My God/Source/Universe/Budda/Allah, whatever it is for you, it is all source energy loves and accepts me just as I am. There is nothing I have to do. I am just finding happiness in being me.

I want self-mastery for others. I came here for a spiritual journey and this is it. I am on it, in it and it is happening. It's time to amp it up.

I clear the resistance from my path, it is an ongoing process.

I release the need to fight and push people away.

I see my light reaching out like branches.

I am asking Spirit/God/Universe to bring the A grade customers to my light. All is well. All the light workers are also bathing with the light I have. All those old souls who are coming back to wipe the slate clean, I am here and I am ready for you and will guide you through the transition.

I see myself juggling clients, five to ten a week.

The benefits of this are that they are all happier and more fulfilled in their lives.

They are telling other people. They are open to changes and they feel healthier in their bodies and in their family units and in their relationships.

My clients are content knowing they are the masters of their own life journey and they are grateful for that. They are happy to give me money and kind words, it makes us all feel great. All is well.

As I become busier I can start to choose my clientele. I chose what days I want to work and my clients are aligned with that. It is my choice to work the days that suit me. I work two days a week and on these days I have back to back clients. I like it this way, it is great. It helps to build momentum and the more clients I see, the more clients are coming.

I book them in over a two day period because it leaves me free days to go away, play music, paint pictures, socialise with friends have an adventure or do what I want to do.

I easily earn enough over these two days to pay my way for the rest of the week, even the rest of the month.

My busy clinic leads to people asking me to do more presentations and talks. I do not have to go looking for it, it comes to me. I get requests for more herbs, more products, more teas, more courses and more information. In fact people want to share with me what I offer.

I am attracting the right type of people to me that is making my life, easy and abundant. I love living my life this way.

I ask source to let the clients come. I am open to receiving more regular clients in my life. All is well in my world.

I take my children on holiday when it suits. We all have a good time. We are creating family fun and making a difference to our family unit. We laugh and laugh on our adventures. Such precious moments.

Wow, I feel quite pumped after writing that!

6.42 P.M.

I have been teaching.

I love teaching and I am so good at it.

I feel good and excited as someone told me that I am the best teacher, which is great to hear. Especially as this is only my second week with this class.

Let me day dream a little.

Students are interested in my detox program and they want to get a copy of my free give away.

It is a great topic and it is a winner. I put it online and it will be live this week, which is good.

In my day dream manifestations I have staff who provide me with all my web input and management.

I love teaching and I am so good at it. It would be great to teach the subjects I like to teach and that I am excited about, rather than the subjects I am selected to. I love it when people come in droves to hear me speak. They love hearing what I have to say.

As I say these visualizations I can feel the excitement growing inside of me. Now this is the work to do.

My 144 subjects are the doorway to this.

In my future what would I like to have?

I have an agent who sorts everything out for me. She sets up all my speaking gigs, does the bookings, takes the bookings as the people come to hear me talk. They then want to buy my books. People love to hear me speak and I offer great content which is inspiring, empowering and interesting. People want more.

It does not take long and the word gets out there. Soon I have gigs all over the world. I choose what places I want to go to. Singapore and Hong Kong are on the list and when I talk here doors open to other space and places.

I still have things that I am going to advertise today as I made a commitment to let others know about the amazing work that I do. So I think today I am going to pick a course to advertise. That sounds like a plan!

Day 11

I have been busy all day.

I had two clients and then two more came in. Woo Hoo.

Things are picking up and I really appreciate that.

This morning I walked up and down the beach saying "I am of value and I radiate my light." I have been seeing my light radiating out more and more. I like saying this affirmation. I find it very uplifting and empowering.

It's time to do a power centre meditation and keep myself aligned. This is what I pretty much believe and it has been working for me.

I have been sorting money things out. Paying the internet bill and paying off debts. Each debt that I pay off makes me feel lighter and lighter. I also had two more herb orders so that is good too. I appreciate this abundance coming into my life.

Maybe that is the end to the diary, he he.

No, I committed to sixty days, so sixty days is what it is.

I decided that I will get the online courses up and running next, that will be my next job.

I have to get ready to do my talk next week. It is time to get it organised and happening. I will get that ready this weekend so I can do a trial run.

I want to talk about the benefits of having my courses. This will be a great exercise.

I have lots of content and I have many educational things to share.

I love the idea of creating one thing once and then being able to sell it over and over again. That is called passive income.

I get my VA and PA to help get some traction and activity on the site and on social media. This gets momentum happening and more business starts to move. I then start to earn passive income, doing something that I love and earning an income whilst I sleep.

There are always more subjects and more courses that I can do. I love writing remarkable content and it is a great way to get my knowledge and information across to others and out there to the world.

People have access to ongoing information that they can continue to use or they can share with others if they so wish.

Teaching and wisdom is one of my natural gifts. It is an innate ability that comes naturally to me. I can share my knowledge over and over again and be able to support myself financially. That feels great.

I love to write so this is a benefit I can share with all. I have a little chat with my VA and see if we can start to advertise some of my courses. I can easily get up to fifty to eighty courses out there that vary in price from being freebies to $100.

Day 12

I have been for a walk and today I was expressing my gratitude's.

I am going to get shit happening today and that feels good to me and feeling good is all that matters.

I am doing a talk tonight which I did previously and it helped me to pick up two new clients last week, as well as two new clients in the last twelve hours. Yipee.

I am seeing my radiance shining. Money is coming into my bank, not sure how much there is, my wages from teaching will start to come in soon as well.

My herbs are busy which is great. I appreciate that.

I was going to spend ten minutes meditating. I will see the radiance come up from the earth and come into my body. This is a good thing. It's time to put me first and for me to be first. I myself in my own authority and in my power. I am a talented writer, healer and teacher and this is okay and enough for me.

Since starting this diary journey the awareness I have had is that it is all about being in alignment and knowing my message. The more I do this, the more business that flows to me and the better my bank balance becomes. It is becoming apparent that focus and commitment are important in creating what we want.

What is alignment you may ask?

That is when we are centred, we are feeling good, we feel connected to source and we are happy. I could explain it as being confident with who I am. It is an increased self-worth which allows me to stay calm amid the storm, to be sure of my direction and focus when confronted my life and it feels strong inside. I hope this explains it.

It is a feeling that I am easily able to distinguish in my body, because I consciously exercise myself to go there and have done so over years of practice.

I did another livestream today, all about connecting.

I have to remember to do a call for action, which is me saying, "if you want to find out more contact me at bla bla." I have to let people know I am open to receiving their business and that I want their custom.

My web guy is always reminding me about the fact that I forget my call for action. Practise will make perfect. It is good to remind myself that I have great value to give others and I do change lives.

Okay?!

Yay, Peace and quiet now, there have been people around. I have no distractions now. That's good.

I am going to ground in my radiance and then go and bank cheques, post herbs and do some work.

I can hear the magpie calling. I better go and feed them.

Day 13

I have $12 in my bank again

The magpie is still calling.

It has decided that this is its home now and he or she is sitting outside the front door and calls for breakfast. I love the call of the Australian magpie. They are so friendly even when they poop on my deck.

After the rush of the sort my shit out day, I am feeling a bit quieter today.

I did not get back to you yesterday. I spent until 8.30 p.m. putting eight courses online. I will put the Raw Food Certificate Course online next and then I will start getting a promo idea started and as for the rest of the courses, I will just keep adding them over time.

I went to get fuel this morning and my card declined. I went shopping on Tuesday and my card declined, plus I have no data on my phone so I was not able to transfer between accounts. I will have to stop watching lots of You Tube on my phone as it uses up the data.

It seems like things have slipped a bit so I will do some manifesting.

I know that our thought patterns can build up momentum and start rolling down the hill. It can also take time to stop this momentum, so it is best I keep it going by seeing the positive future I am choosing to create.

I did my feminine presence meditation and I feel grounded and connected now. I see this as something vital and I think it is what needs to happen after walking the dogs in the morning. The best way to do this meditation is with music.

Males created meditation practises where we sit still in silence. As females, we are all about movement and flow, so moving mediations can be quite powerful for us.

I am going to look into listening to music and finding some more feel good music. I do love music and singing.

I am going to do a livestream about connecting again after this. This is part two as I had so much to say and I want to keep my recordings short and sweet.

I can now look at having a weekly topic which I can research and explore each week.

Okay where was I?

Manifesting......

I have done my gratitude down the beach the last few days so I will write about other things I desire in my life.

What would it be like to have ten clients a week? Let's go there in present time.

I am so busy now that I have to juggle the clients around and I am getting to the point where I will raise my prices.

I have had enough of clients being scattered all over the place. I want then to be in three days of the week, no negotiations.

As Tuesday is teaching days, my client days are Monday after 12 pm, Wednesday and Friday.

The clients that I have are great.

I have regular repeats, plus new clients. New clients are referrals from my regular clients. A lot of them are working through my seven steps of my Higher Laws Program which are ongoing.

There is always more to do.

Some people like the fact that they are their own master and their own doctor. My clients are learning to connect to themselves and to know how to drive their own life. They are learning to tap into their inner genius and start to live their lives according to their gifts. It is easier once we know what our gifts are.

I see people telling others, "Just get onto Louise's Programs, it is great. She is so supportive and she easily helps you to get on track. She is great at helping you to find direction and start achieving your passions and your goals. Her program is fabulous and it has really helped me so much. I love how I feel now and my life has changed so much."

"I love how I feel now and how my life has changed. I have more presence and this has changed many outcomes in my life, especially my relationship. I have so much love and joy in my life now. I feel like I have awakened my body, my cells, my DNA, and the light I have on my body."

My clients tell others and others notice how different these people look and feel and how they are very happy and are constantly smiling. This is how the ripples have spread.

I juggle the clients around and I fit them in. I tell myself that once I am up to fifteen a week then I will put my prices up or even double them.

Good for me. I could even raise my prices now.

I am going off to finish some jobs. It's so cold I have gloves on whilst I am writing.

I will be hopefully changing my website this week. Online platforms here I come. I will have to find out what people are searching and looking for. That is a plan.

Ha ha, that's another livestream. I am sticking to schedule.

Day 14

Woohoo I have $12.30 in the bank.

I had a client this morning. Herb and client money has not come through yet. That's the nature of the game.

What is good is that I am feeling OK about it. I have not been worry at all. I have been doing this and that and have not been pushing myself or working hard today.

I decided to sit here and write some info from books.

I have lots of books. I used to have half a sea container full of books and I had to thin them out when I moved interstate. I like books, which only makes sense that I like to write them.

I got my 144 topic written up and I am starting to go through my talk which I am doing on Wednesday.

This morning I chanted two lots of one hundred chants. 'I am valued and I am rewarded for my value.'

The other one I did was 'I am rewarded for my gifts with money.' I did one hundred of both. I am dedicated to changing my financial situation.

I had a friend ring me up and she is going to do a video interview with me on the 17th of this month which is good. I will use this as a manifestation tool as well.

Let's do some manifestation.

People see my interview and it creates a spark that becomes ignited.

People contact me and ask for an interview. I get a phone call asking me if I have time to have a chat, of course I say "Sure."

When I do this they offer me some contracting or consulting work, without tying me into a fixed contract.

The consulting is for a large company that loves to care for the wellbeing of their staff and they know and understand the value of looking after staff. They are aware that they get better efficiency and productivity from them when they are healthy and happy. They want to keep their staff happy and so do I. I teach them about health, wellbeing, nutrition and all about strategies that we can use to practise self-care and be happy.

I get asked to come and do some talks in different locations over Melbourne and Australia. They offer to pay me $5,000 for an afternoon, which I am happy to so, though only for now.

This is great because it increases my mailing list extensively and it also increases my client base, of which I am charging optimum fees.

People want a piece of what I have to say and this is great as I am able to sell more books, courses and products.

They love the books so much that the company says, 'Let's buy one of these books and give them to all staff members.' We are all extremely joyous about that. It is a win win situation.

I am very happy about this for a number of reasons.

Primarily people are increasing their awareness and are starting to communicate better with their family, work colleges and friends. They also are more conscious about their behaviour or thoughts and they are choosing to act, think and feel much more positive, proactive and empowered. Another bonus is that my financial status is becoming extremely secure now.

I have to ask the publisher for another run of the books, Woo Hoo I am laughing and loving this ride.

I feel like my business is rocking and that's great. I have worked hard for this and I have everything lined up and I am prepared for success. My money caps are increased and I am open to receiving much more now. Life is really comfortable for me now.

Money is coming in I am deciding to invest in my future and secure some assets. I choose to invest my finances in things that have value, transparency, morals and are supporting our environment and is really helping people. I have enough income now to be able to tilth ten percent of my income.

I create weekend seminars for those in need.

I find people who are depressed, anxious, lost or who are struggling. I find women and men who have been abused and who have lived with the effects of abuse. I attract people to me who have not had the opportunity in their lifetime to be given the knowledge and support that they needed to make sound choices in their life that will benefit and empower them. I give them the tools and opportunity to turn their lives around.

I screen the people to see if they are motivated for change as I know that people have to be ready and willing to be in a space to be open to receiving such opportunity.

I sort of feel like Robin Hood. I am earning from the rich and giving to the poor. It is such a satisfying feeling and I love the support that I get in return. This is a real feel good space.

In fact this feels so good that it starts a movement which is excellent. People start to share the same kind of Robin Hood process. And so the ripple spreads, on and on and out and out.

I love this manifestation, it is great.

It feels so good and could well be a reality one day.

Everything and anything is possible.

It just takes one great opportunity to be taken and one good lead from the right person who believes in the mission and the vision and who has the ability to be a co-creator in this.

This is lift off!

Day 15

Still the same bank amount, though money is flowing in and out now.

I was out in the city today for a family outing.

We went to the city, to the Victoria markets and then to ACMI.

This is the Australian Centre of Moving Images. We then went to a 'Wallace and Gromit' exhibition. I had some cash and I decided we can have a day out. This has been one of my wishes to take my family out for more outings. I love family days.

I am sitting in the car with my youngest son and I am explaining my diary and why I am writing it. We are both sitting in the back seat and we are going to manifest together. My son is twelve.

We are both seeing me working and having a good job with a good income with plenty of time for doing what we want to do.

In that time we are doing fun family things like tree surfing, going out for dinner, going away for the weekends, seeing friends, going to the movies or the drive in's.

We are eating healthy food, what we want when we want. We like to eat healthy organic food and business is doing well so we buy some lovely real salmon, not that farmed stuff and we can buy an entire fish. We slice it up and put it in the freezer. We are eating yummy raw organic chocolate, the brands that we like best. We do not have to think about the choices we have to make with eating, we eat what we want.

As we have free choices we are free to do fun things. Fun things include watching movies together, going for walks, having baking days and eating Thai food.

We have time for the whole family to come together and we eat together. We are treating the family and are buying presents, having days out and eating cake while we are out.

We get a ferry from home to Geelong and it's great. We go to the water park that is in Geelong. We have lots of holidays, boating skiing, picnicking, learning to do new stuff, hot air ballooning and all the family is coming. We are even Sky diving and going to unusual and new places.

What a great manifestation we created together.

Day 16

$220 in the bank and a bill for $190

I am feeling crappy today.

It's very cold and I do not feel very positive.

I feel quite overwhelmed with my 'To Do' list. I have a list of over twenty things.

So what I normally do is keep working and pushing myself to do more. I keep pushing and pushing. It is not a good space and it is like I work hard and crash hard.

I want to look and explore what I do and how I am organising my time.

What is urgent and important?

Well my family is always number one. Providing food and healthy shelter is urgent and important, after all I have to feed everyone.

What is urgent and not important?

Answering emails I suppose. I think I feel this is urgent, when in reality it is not. I could change how I feel about that.

What is not important and not Urgent?

Social media and scrolling through Facebook is a definite. Playing games and watching TV is also here. These can all be traps for me that take time. All my spam and junk email can also go in

75

here, one thing about being a business and putting yourself out there, people want to ride off your back or send you lots of junk and spam.

The final quadrant is the important and not urgent. What comes in here?

I think this could be the most important quadrant to explore.

Here I am networking, having quality time for me or my family. I am sorting out daily emails, meditation, music, dancing, exercise and being grateful. This looks like a great list and maybe I can start to focus more attention here.

I did go to singing group this morning and then I spent time tidying things up.

Tomorrow is a full moon, so its crazy times again. I often find I am more wide awake on a full moon. Sometimes the moon can be so bright it wakes me up as it shines through the windows.

I think I will be spending time today doing what I 'should' be doing not what I want to be doing. I am not a fan of the word should. Could is a much better word. What could I do today?

That changes my mood. The push to be doing what I ought to be doing is not always what I like to do or does it make me happy. Instead I would rather have fun.

It is also cold and this gets to me down. I have been in this state of Australia for five years and at the end of each winter I get the winter blues. I had a couple of weeks in Hawaii early on, so another month away in a warm climate during a cold winter would be great.

I feel disconnected today and this is why I am not doing stuff that requires presence such as livestreams and shining my knowledge. There is no point pushing or pretending to be something that I am not, as there is no integrity in there.

So how can I change my mindset?

I could go for a run, have a sleep, meditate, scream, punch, and jump about.

I do not even feel up to that, even though it would warm me

up. I will do a five minute power meditation, though first I will see myself warm.

I am in Bali and it's lovely up here in the mountains. It's not too humid and there are often cooling showers later in the afternoon. I feel warm and I feel the warmth right down to my bones. It is also not too hot to make it uncomfortable to sleep.

What I like about being here is the fact I like to eat more fruit and raw foods. The warmer weather makes me want to choose cooler foods. I have a nice cold fridge full of coconut water, mangosteens, huge passion fruit, pawpaw, banana, mandarins, plus other fruits that I do not even remember the names.

I have my own little scooter that takes me down to the beach, I know where the quieter spots are and on this side of the mountain driving is easy and there are less tourists and more locals.

I stop to have some lunch at a Balinese restaurant on the side of the road. I love to eat where the locals eat and eating chicken and fish here feels good as its local and not farmed.

I love visiting the beach and swimming in the warm water here. I also love the Balinese people and their kind and friendly nature.

It's a great place to spend a month and get away from the winter blues.

7.35 P.M.

I did not stop and I ended up smashing through my 'To Do' list.

I got lots of things done on my list. I write a list every Sunday and Monday and that gives me my weekly 'To Do' list. It felt good getting some of these things off my shoulders.

It keeps me accountable and on track of working and this is important as I work for myself. I have to keep myself actually doing work, though sometimes I can do too much.

Now... let's go do some manifesting.

I have my own masseuse. In fact I have four, as I like to receive a different type of massage or therapy on different days.

One is deep tissue massage, one is relation massage and one who just helps me to relax and let go. The last one is my myotherapist who helps to works specifically on certain aches and pains on the body.

I love being able to choose my body worker whenever and how ever I feel depending on what I believe my body will benefit with today. In fact I now have four therapists, one for four days of the week. I call this pamper time.

I love being able to spend my time having therapy. I love being pampered and having choice. I know my therapists are there for me and I trust them explicitly as I am one of their best regular customers and we have an excellent connection. I no longer have clients of my own because I do not have to.

My therapists like to therapize me. I send them lots of clients and I pay them well as I value their services. I keep coming back or rather they actually come to me. It is much easier for me that way and I am happy to pay for that service. We have mutual respect and value for each other.

So I will give some gratitude for today, as when I do this for a few days I feel good.

I appreciate having my bathroom almost finished and soon being able to have a shower.

I also appreciate singing group. I love singing and it always makes me feel good, even if some of the songs bring tears to my eyes.

I also appreciate feeling warm now, and that is good, as I like feeling good.

Okay, it's time to unpack the word sovereign. This is one of the words in my message language.

What does it mean? Let me see.

Part of my message is about stepping into your own sovereignty. This is you being in your supreme power of personal authority.

Words that resonate here are ascendency, domination, supremacy, power, authority, control, influence, rules, and regiment. It is a state of self-governing. Here you have the full right and power as your own governing body over itself, without interference from outside sources or bodies.

The state of sovereignty is internalisation law. You are your own supreme law making authority. You are your own monarch and you have found your own honour. Basically you make up the rules to your life and do, be and have what you want.

I like this word and I believe we are all born to step into our sovereign right. You can see that I researched some of its meanings in a dictionary.

If some of these words seem a little controlling, I mean it in the sense of you being in charge and making your own rules that fulfil you and make you happy. You bring empowered to be yourself. It is refreshing to not have to watch what you say, when you say it and to whom you say it.

Day 17

I have about $400 in my account, woo hoo.

I still have payments to come in, Air B N B and wages. I am rocking it today.

I have a little room downstairs. Just a little studio or bedsit, it is commonly rented out one night a week, as I am eight minutes' drive away from the local hot springs.

I paid my overdue rates, next is my tax and the website. It feels great being able to chip off my debts and pay my bills.

I was thinking just then of running some FB ads for the herb website.

To do that it might mean I will have to tidy up the website. It needs some time on it. Some of the pictures are missing and there are not full descriptions and pictures for all the teas. It needs time, though it never seems to be priority. I am sure it will get attended to at some time.

I opened an Instagram account for the herbs today and posted a picture on it. The picture looks great. I posted some pictures of herbs to help with leaky gut and for lead toxicity and I got a response which is great. It seems that for some reason the herbs are working for me. I like that, I like playing with the herbs.

Today I will go and manifest about my herb business then.

I have a great little herb business. Herbs are coming in and out and that is always a great sign of business.

I have two staff members that are helping me run the business. A junior staff member that does the bagging up and getting the orders ready and the other person does the marketing, helping with customer satisfaction, advertising, ordering and bringing in the new leads.

The staff do not need me which is great, they run it all themselves, as they know what needs to be done. I listen to their suggestions and they come up with some excellent ideas.

Admin Andy (the name for the marketer) says "Let's change the branding" and I say

"Sure" and off we go.

They both help to update the website and make it look fabulous. It looks professional, the photos look amazing and I love the look of it.

Suggestions they come up with are advertising options, permanent ads that work, colours, photos, packaging, benefits for regular customers etc. I love their suggestions.

Together all three of us get the business pumping. I love the idea of having someone help blend and pack, though I do like the packing and sending of the herbs myself at times. This is a great idea.

We expand and expand, though just at the right times and not beyond our means. I have been there and learnt that one before. I allow this business to grow slowly, as it is important to now grow beyond your means. I had a retail shop, a wholefood organic raw cafe and I expanded too soon and it cost me a lot financially. I have learned my lesson there. I know this now and I feel it is in my blood and my veins. I know when it is appropriate to change.

It is good people are getting fed up using doctors drugs, not getting the results they want and they are looking for more natural options other things. After all we have been using herbs since the beginning of time. People like my information about herbs and they are willing to give new things a try.

People like to learn how herbs can help them and I have plenty of information to give them. I give them more blogs, more courses, more information and more education. Educated people can make informed choices.

The website shows herb courses, herb workshops, her seminars, herb blogs and articles. It also has testimonials, reviews and great feedback. It is all there for them to see and do. It is becoming a bigger and bigger thing every week.

It is the plant family with their plant business.

It's all good things and it grows like a healthy plant. I would love for one of my children to become involved in this growing business and from this we create a successful family empire.

They give me lists of jobs to do to help with promotion until they are able to take on the role themselves.

"Mum can you write copy for this, can you write a blog about that?" They ask me.

I trust their direction because it feels good. So it has now become a family business and I love it. Yee Har.

I must have another order in my inbox by now.

Laters, I am feeling good now.

12.30 P.M.

I have to do a newsletter today.

I have to be mindful about my headlines. I learnt that the Headline sells and the sub-headline tells.

I know to make the headline something that will attract attention. It can be something people dislike and something that will resonate with them.

Feeling overworked, overwhelmed and under paid will resonate with lots of people. This would be an urgent want for people. Urgent wants are good ideas for attracting attention.

I rarely use subhead lines, though there often is a little heading on the newsletter templates that I use.

I wonder whether the videos reach more people than the emails. I did learn about the newsletter topics that will engage people.

1. "What the Fuck?" is something that can blow people away and be filled of crazy facts and figures
2. Lightning bolt is powerful and straight to the point.
3. Factual proof information, this can be like 'Did you know?'
4. A story, we all love a story now don't we
5. Focusing on the pain, what is the pain that these people and my clients have. I know I can focus on that.
6. Transformation, this can be a story of a breakthrough event or adventure

These are some examples of what I could use.

So, what am I in the mood for? I think a good story. Let me think of one, there are many.

11.15 P.M.

I just got home. I went to a full moon drumming night.

There is a lot happening globally at this time. We are half way through a seventy year shift on this planet and we are just about half way through that. This halfway point is about steeping into the new now.

I like to use the analogy that it is time to walk through the door to change and as we do that it is good to turn our back on things in our life that do not serve us or help us. In fact we can even shut the door behind us and say goodbye to the old. It's time to turn your back on the dramas, things that do not serve you and things in your life that do not feel good.

We have an eclipse tonight and one on the 21st of this month, which is in about two weeks.

It is a paramount time for change, so in the next two weeks

83

it is an ideal time to look at what you want to change, as the next eighteen years could pivot our future world that we live in, one way or another. What way would you chose?

Soooo.......... I am going to up my success rants and see myself shining and radiating more and more.

More and More.

The light is being powered in. I am open to receiving the new in my life. I give value from the heart and I let in everything that serves me for my highest and greatest good.

Day 18

I have $190 in the bank
Busy day today.

I did my first talk to get some of the bugs out of the course and presentation that I want to do.

I spent nearly all day, making the presentation, writing and printing the handouts. I did the presentation this evening to four people and it was good and it went well.

I have to do the slide show and book some dates, maybe one in the city and one in Frankston. I will see what is available. I can then book more talks and then two dates for the extended weekend course. It sounds like a plan to do these talks over two venues and locations as it will be some great market research. I will make some enquiries.

Apart from that I was busy. One client contact me and I have a freebie client tomorrow and I need to make some phone calls. Tomorrow will focus on my public speaking opportunities.

So what can I focus energy on today?

Where the attention goes, energy flows.

I will manifest how I would like my speaking life to be.

I see many talks happening. They are now a regular occurring thing. I chose to have small groups with ten to fifteen people there and they are keen to learn more. I like these small intimate groups. I allow my intuition to guide me to where I can find these people. People want to learn. I have created my list of people who want to learn and want to do this.

I create some great copy that helps to share with people what 'The Higher Laws' is about and it sparks interest. I have a growing group. The weekends are a success with ten people coming which is great. That is $30,000 for the weekend minus the venue.

I am laughing and I enjoy it. All is well.

People love to hear what I have to say, they love my knowledge and mastery to life. I have a great website that is working well. It is good and it is happening for me.

I share my knowledge easily. I know how to budget and what to do. In fact I do not need to sell myself, the content that I have sells itself.

I am blubbering as I have had a big day. No meditation today, it's been rush, rush, rush.

Onwards and upwards guys n gals.

Day 19

I have $85 in the bank and waiting for wages coming in
As I am writing this I realised that I said that I was waiting.
What am I waiting for?

It's time to stop waiting. It is time to get out there.

It is a time to start being and doing rather than waiting. This needs activity. I am glad I picked myself up on that.

I did not get to do any meditation again today. That is not helping or working for me if I do not take the time to centre and align myself.

On a lighter note, I did learn how to do my own buffer posts on my social media network.

I did my 144 topic this week, recorded it and did a great video. I am saving the mp3's. Not sure what I will do with them, I will just save them for now.

I then had a client who helped me get the loan to clear my final debts from previous business ventures of growing too soon, too fast. As I said I have learnt that one.

That was not that long ago, only a few years.

I got the last course up and running as well today.

A friend in the past helped me to create a freebie funnel give away to source more email addresses. It did not work as no one signed up for anything. Not sure about that either. I obviously have to change the copy, which is the wording and see how that goes.

I have had business failures in the past, though I also carried on and have been persistent. Six months ago I did not know the difference between sales and marketing and now I do. I know I am learning so much about business management.

I have a coaching session tomorrow so I have a few things to ask and sort out.

I created a social media spreadsheet to help me to be more consistent in my advertising, marketing and what I am doing.

I am also learning and finding out what people are looking for and this helps me to write good copy or adverting material.

9.55 P.M.

I was distracted with dinner so I had to stop writing.

I will explore my success in my future as my writing focus today.

Being a successful business woman means I have the time and the lifestyle that I want. It does not necessarily mean I am rich and wealthy. It is more about life quality and choice.

It is about the freedom to do what I want and the freedom to make the choices I want.

My manifesting helps me to have the time to do what I want. Having more clients and financial freedom means I can pay a cleaner who comes to my house once a week or even twice a week. This is great as it gives me time to spend with my family and to do more things for me.

Having more time for me is great and I have half a day a week to do some creative things like art, ceramics, making things, sewing, and oil painting. I have time for things that feel good. It makes me feel good doing crafts and having time for me. It is a great expressive outlet.

I have time to socialise, time for a cuppa with friends, time to go shopping, time for walking in the bush and on the beach, time for going out, time for dinner, time for music, time for fun, time for family activities, time for reading, time for relaxing, time for friskiness, time for great sex, time for beautification, time for pampering, time for nurturing, time for nourishment, time for getting some yummy food, time for laughter, time for joy, time for gratitude, time for presence, time for connection to others, time for love, time for discovery, time for exploration, time for empowerment, time for success, and time for growing my tribe.

I have divine timing.

Day 20

Today is a day for completion.

Finish the bathroom, finish copy for the higher laws and copy for the online courses.

I am taking my son to deb practice tonight.

11.27 A.M.

Today I have been learning about split campaigns and it is doing my head in so I am having a break.

I learnt about the fact that 90% of what we think in our daily 60,000 to 70,000 thoughts are repeated thoughts from the day before.

This makes so much sense and can be a reason why so many of us are in default mode. Therefore….. What does make sense is that it is important to keep bringing new positive thoughts in and this could be why my hundred chants or affirmations are working for me. I am taking time each day to bring in new positive thoughts to replace my default ones.

It is vital to bring new ideas and thoughts in if you want to change where you are at. So I will do just that.

I am living with my ten clients a week and this is working well for me.

I allocate time to do my clients, Monday arvo's, Wednesday and Fridays are my clinic days. My clients also want herbs as well which is a bonus. This gives me more income and exposure. Business is looking and feeling great.

I connect with my clients, I do healings, hair analysis, in fact it does not matter what I do, as I just do it. I like looking after my client base. I have got my clients in from social media, advertising and word of mouth.

I teach them to connect to their bodies, minds, emotions and spiritual selves. I teach them alignment and this is easy as I do this often and have been doing this to help my successful business gain momentum.

Having $1,000 a week from my clients is great and this is only the beginning.

I earn more from the extras that come in as well. I am saving money on a regular basis and I am off to Hawaii in two weeks as I balance my hard work with relaxing play and I paid for this trip in just a couple of weeks. In fact I was able to book it and pay for it just like that. It was a real off the cuff thing.

I love having this freedom.

When I go over there I make some headway in regards to my writing career. I like it and it feels good.

My little excursions have also led to a trip to Bali to sort out some lose ends there. This is great as I have been wanting to sort this lose end out now for a few years and have not had the finances to do so.

I meet with amazing connections over there and we make arrangements and sort agreements. It opens new opportunities for me. I am able to easily talk and communicate with the people that I need to. This gives me a great sense of relief. I got word out to the person that I needed to communicate with and told him I was on my way and he complied with my wishes.

I bring with me my new desires and I understand how good it is to move forward. I like letting go of these lose ends. Things are always working out for me now. There may be some pebbles and rocks on the road, though I know how to hurdle over them or side track them.

All my Australian debts are also paid off. These are debts from courses I have attended and payment plans that I have been on. Some of them have been going on for years. I repay my loan as well. It's not a huge loan, though it is all gone now.

All my small debts are cleared and gone. This is a great feeling.

Life is giving me choices now and I like having the freedom to choose. I choose no more debts and paying things off. I either have the finances to do it and I do it, or I don't. This makes it all very easy. The first choice I choose now that there is plenty of money coming in for me is to clear all my debts.

I like the choices I make to transcribe my books. I have choice in life and I know which project is the most important for me to choose first.

My books keep rolling out now I have financial assistance for editing. The book publishing process becomes easier and easier over time.

Today I am one third of the way through this diary and it's great. It is good in the fact that I do not seem to worry like I was before.

I have a much more relaxed view. I have a goal, I have a plan and I am taking action and most of all I love it.

This week I would like to step up my presence in everything that I do.

I did not contact places for speaking engagements, though I did finish other stuff today which was good.

I am going to read my dramatic texts I received from last night. This is another story, though I am not going there today. I put the phone under the couch as I did not want to hear the bling of the phone.

This just makes me more determined to spend more time on this diary. I want that 90% of yesterday's thoughts to be reduced.

The more I focus on what I want and new life choices and experiences, the less time my thoughts are in default. New thoughts each day and if I consciously choose to take the time to do, act or behave in a different and more positive way it will create the desired outcome over time.

11.50 P.M.

Today was a very interesting day.

I have allowed my personal life to get in the way of my positive frame of mind and this in turn affects my ability to manifest clients and attract things of value in my life.

Instead I let things make me feel shit, so I reached for the wine. I feel quite angry and hurt and the way that I dealt with the situation at home. I will work harder and keep myself busy and away from distractions and temptations.

I cleaned and tidied, drove my son to where he had to go and then came back and did some more. In the end I started doing a puzzle and watched comedy movies to try and raise my spirits, until we had to go and pick up my son.

I figured after lunch that there was no point pretending I was not feeling shit or even to push against how I feel, so instead I decided to chill with the puzzle and funny movies.

I had worked hard all week and had completed a lot of stuff so having some down time is okay. I have to keep telling myself if I am not doing something worthy or productive then that is all right. I do not have to be achieving and working all the time. I believe I am not doing anything at all when I am relaxing and I have to change that outlook. It has taken time for me to be okay with having time out.

Guilt can be such a bugger and it can easily stop us having fun and moving forward.

Now I am in bed. I have been waking up early and I am wide awake at 6am or even earlier. It is very dark at that time in winter. Because I am wide awake I just get up. I figure there is no point just sitting in bed. This is a good time for me to write as the house is quiet.

Tomorrow I am off to earth church and this morning I did have a little jog on the beach. I was aware of being a little out of breath the last time I was on the dance floor, so hopefully this will motivate me to run some more. That sounds like a good plan. Even if I only run round the block, I will just make sure it a small block.

I know that my body is a tool and a vessel and I will help it to feel happier and healthier as much as I can. In turn it will look after me.

My body is a vital component for alignment and to be honest the only thing stopping or blocking me from moving forward right now is my personal life. I will sleep on it and ponder the situation in the morning.

I can say some more positive statements or affirmations after writing. I find this is a good time as well. Early in the morning or last thing at night works best.

I did two times one hundred suggestions this morning and I was feeling good then.

'I release the need to be heard and I am important,' I can do that one hundred times, along with 'I love me and I am important.'

That always helps to raise my vibration.

Good night.

Day 21

I believe there is about $55 in the bank.

I slept okay, though I dreamt I was in a chemistry lab and I was making herbal preparations.

My ears are ringing this morning as I have had some extra stress the last few days and then I tend to eat crap food or not at all. It is time to step up my health and start to get serious about it. Self-care and self-healing is part of moving up to the next level. New levels new devil.

My mind is quite shattered and I want to focus.

I was just saying to myself 'I am focused, I am focused.' I think I did it three times and then my mind wandered off. That could be funny.

I started again I think I got up to five times before my mind wandered off. I think the best thing to do is to do a focus wheel.

Have you ever done a focus wheel? You write a circle in the middle and you put the thing that you want, though you do not have yet. Then you fill the clock wheel with twelve true happening statements. The aim is to create time where you focus on the good things in your life and see how it reflects back on what you want.

Not sure if that makes sense so I will write one now.

What is it that I want in the middle of my wheel?

It is best being something I want and am not quite there with it yet.

In the middle of my wheel there is 'I am a successful business woman.'

The next stage is to write the twelve things around the clock wheel which are good feeling and happening things.

Focus wheel here we go.

1. Things are always working out for me
2. I love being financially secure and free
3. I love the living the lifestyle that I want, travelling, writing, warm weather, speaking and teaching.
4. I am established and recognised in my field of expertise
5. I am easily doing the rinse and repeat, rinse and repeat in my business
6. My success gives me the choices that I want in life
7. I value freedom in my life
8. I love moving forward and I follow what works easily for me
9. My speaking arena expands on a weekly and monthly basis
10. Publishers ask me to publish with them
11. My mental attitude is one of success, freedom, happiness and flow
12. I love feeling good. Nothing is more important than feeling good.

There you go, I have spent time focusing on the good things in my life and I feel my spirits have be raised already.

I am ready to go bush walking now, off I go.
Today is a new day. Today I will livestream. I am happy and free.
Today I will do my 144 recording on the 'Amazing Body.'
Today I am focused on flow, alignment and following the radiance.
Today things are working out for me. Today I have the answers.
Today life unfurls for me. Today I am free.

Today I cut cords and let go of what is not serving me. Today I am free to be me and that is fine. Today my higher self loves and accepts me just as I am. In fact my higher self loves and accepts me just as I am every day.

4 P.M.

Back again.

I came to a conclusion today. This journey is all about me shining my radiance and enjoying my life.

This is the most important thing for me to do.

Just be aligned and just see that golden radiance shine out.

I was listening to someone talk about courage today and he said that a true master is one who can get the perfect balance. Balance is always so important. Anything in lack or excess can put us out of balance.

I could be some wonderful 'love and peace' person who is always nice, loving and compassionate, though that is not really real. We all have good days and shit days. Though it also has to balance out with everyday living, being a mum, paying the bills, sorting the kids, and so it goes on. No good having my head in the clouds if my feet are not on the ground.

My aim therefore is to find the radiance and let the radiance shine. I will do what it takes to allow myself to shine. When I use the word time I mean I a lit up and I am ignited. I have the sparkle in my eyes and I am excited about where I am leading myself to.

Alignment and centring that sparkle is paramount and I am focusing on doing just that.

So my radiance shines so light that people want to be in it.

Light is the be all and end all, as the saying goes.

It shines over the darkness and when we walk in the dark and shine the light, it illuminates our way.

My goodness that is so cliché.

Shine on, shine on.

Day 22

I imagine there is still $55 in the bank
I am wide awake again
Not sure if it is the Lions Gate which is the earth shifts that are happening now or the full moon, either way, I am awake. I will use the time to write and manifest.

I still keep thinking about the fact that 90% of the thoughts that we have are repeated from the day before. This is a huge awareness to me. It means that so many people are just going round and round regurgitating the same thoughts day after day. It is just like ground hog day.

I will bring in some new thoughts.

I love being of value to people.

It feels great when clients knock at my door and want to come and see me. I like or even love my skill, intellect and ability to see and understand what is the underlying things that are happening for them. I know that I have this gift and I know that it is my time.

I now know it is time to get my message out there now that it is clear. I can allow it to grow from there.

I see myself being showered by my radiance. I breathe in golden light.

Yesterday when I was at Earth Church I got insight about how the light shines on the leaves and how the sun comes up over the horizon and how it tips the top leaves of the tree first and then it heads down. To get the early light, we have to reach up for it. We have to grow towards it to be bathed in it the longest.

Last night I sat and saw my higher self and she was looking at me.

She said "I love you and I accept you just the way that you are."

It was a memorable experience and it brought tears to my eyes because I could see her face and feel her love and acceptance.

It is reassuring to know that there is a part of me and loves and accepts me at all times and in every situation.

More amazing, happy and joyous new thoughts come with that feeling. I love knowing I have amazing talents that help people. I see people benefiting from these abilities, time and time again.

It's great knowing I can fix and help heal others. I know I have the gift of healing and facilitating people through the changes in their lives.

I can write and I love to write and I will be a published author again. It is easy and it is time to move forward with that that.

I change my mentor to be in keeping with my success. I am in a space where I can let my divine guidance coach me through life using the avenue of the earth church.

I was thinking of my coach just then. I know that there is always more and there are easier ways to bring in the leads and connections. When we work with a coach who is successful in what it is that we wish to achieve, they teach us things that they know how to do. We learn quicker from those who have already done it. It is a great way to speed things up.

There are new things coming my way and things are always working out for me.

I am going to manifest my family herb business as it felt so good last time.

One of my children has chosen in their adult space to become involved in my herb business.

It starts with us as having small orders and then it goes up. We get more and more orders each week, six times a week, ten times a week, twenty times a week and even thirty times a week. It keeps growing and growing and we see the sales increasing.

People love using herbs and they are becoming more and more interested in natural cures that do not harm the body. These people are able to find me easily on my lovely updated website.

This is great. We have run split campaigns for over three months now and we are starting to work out what advertising campaigns are working and those that are not.

All is well.

The momentum has started and new things are becoming noticed all the time. It is great to see. I love using herbs and herbs love me using them. That is a great thing. It will just expand and expand and I love that I have someone in the family to share the rewards with. Someone who wants this business to succeed, someone to help pack and stack and someone to pack, print and send. This feels really good. It is a pleasant job playing with the herbs.

I am open to receiving new ways of adding choice in my life and increasing value in my life.

My heart is open to receiving and I am seeing the flow coming in.

I change the paradigm of my old ways and I welcome the new ideas and decisions that I make in my life.

Day 23

Not sure what is happening in my bank
I am hoping that my wages are in there.
I am still waking up early in the dark.
I get up and write and sort of feel I am downloading stuff. I am finishing a Sci Fi romance fiction novel.

I am open to having a story for my 144 topics. I like to use my life experiences and stories to help get my message across, so universe I am open to remembering an inspiring and exciting story.

Things do not come to us in our lives unless we ask for it, so it is very important to ask.

When we ask for help it is like we are putting an open transmitter out there. When we ask we open our hearts to receptive mode.

Many times in the past I have felt lost and then I end up asking for help. I make a booking to see a therapist or someone who can help and as soon as I do that I start to get my answers. Learn to ask for what you want and to tell others about it.

I want fun
I want joy
I want peace
I want happiness
I was listening to something the other day about intent and how

science is proving our thoughts play out in our lives and create our lives. We now have scientific proof that our thoughts are creating reality!

I was asking for some help with marketing and a friend of my daughters offered to come and help me set something up. I feel like it is coming together.

I am going to set some intent.

It is my intent to have my herbal business flourish, it is my intent to have my clientele flourish. I will have ten clients a week and I am out and about seeing more people.

This is my intent and I know that the universe will do whatever it needs to create that.

It will mould and shape the matter. I see it moving forward all around me as my message and my intent is clear. People want to come and they are attracted to my words, my energy and my vibration.

People are attracted to my gifts, my healing abilities and they see themselves being drawn to the light. They will say things like I was feeling shit and I was asking for help and then I saw your add. Your words came up and they just resonated with me, so I had to come and see you. I am grateful for this.

I appreciate the work that I am doing. I see everything being great, I am feeling very excited about my future and I am happy. Things have really changed for me now. I am so grateful for your help and support, so much so that I am going to share it with others.

I see the energy forming and bringing the right people to me at the right time.

These people are attracted to where I am adverting or sharing my information. I see it moulding and shaping the universe, as the universe brings it all together.

I have 100% intent and focus. I ask my innate to allow my healing energy to radiate and attract the right people who are wanting and are ready for change. These people are in a situation to easily pay for it.

Universe, please help with my request.

1.30 P.M.

$88 in the bank still no wages.

I am on the train and I am on my way to weekly teaching.

It is bloody cold.

I have been thinking about the fact that we now have scientific proof about the power of intent and the fact that they are creating a machine to see and track that.

I put up a Facebook add and it had reached forty people by noon. This is for me to track every twelve hours. When it reaches a certain number I plan to change the wording of the post and then run it again. This will help me work out what copy is working for me.

I can change the heading and then see how quickly that gains the same numbers. This is a way to track and see what works best and in the end what can be most cost effective when it comes to advertising.

I want to be able to consciously mould matter and see that there is a person who has invested in my herbs who suddenly has seen my add and they say

"Yes, I want to learn how to make my own herb teas. I could create my own de-stress teas all of my very own."

How great would that be?

They start to browse and to read my info and they see that I have lots of information, support and help to offer. They look to see what else they can add to their repertoire.

This is an example of how a small sale can lead into something a lot bigger or even ongoing.

This is why small sales are always acceptable and important.

People who want herbs can see my site and they can buy small amounts of herbs anytime. These small sales can easily lead into bigger sales, after all our best customers are our current customers.

6.55 P.M.

Not sure what is in the bank, I gave up waiting for my wages to come in.

I started the day early today and I am

I was manifesting on the train and thinking about how I was feeling. This morning my higher self was looking at me again and telling me that she loves me just as I am and that she has always been there for me and she always will.

Then I started visualising how good it is going to feel and to have my own assistants and team to help on our vision. It will be fabulous.

She will say to me "Would you like me to tidy this up?" and I will say "Sure thing, thanks for that, it would be excellent.

I will have feelings of relief because it will bring lots of feelings of relief because it will free me up to do the things that I want to do which will be great.

She will say "Let me do this and let me do that" or "I am going off to do this and that" and off she goes. (I am pretending that my assistant is a she, sexist I know, though I feel in my heart it will be a she).

No more sorting through emails, as she does all that for me. No more spending time typing things up, she will also do that. No more following up with phone calls as she does that to. It is great.

I give her course content and off she will go sorting it out, reading, editing and tidying it up. I also give her material to proof read and she does that too. There is no need to do or say anything, she knows the system now. She totally gets it.

Another bonus is that she often works from home as I do not need her onsite. This makes it easy and it is fabulous for both of us.

She communicates easily and brings in lots more leads. She is great at bringing in more people in to our events.

How does this feel for me? It feels very yummy.

I have always been great at seeing what is happening as I have powerful insight and intuition. I want to emphasize how I feel in this diary as it is good to write it down and to see it in black and white.

I feel

- Relief
- Excitement
- Ease
- Appreciative
- Grateful
- Inspired
- Blessed
- Relieved
- Creative
- Expressive
- Expansive
- Abundant
- Happy
- Joyful
- Delighted
- Understood
- Awakened
- Grounded
- Centred
- Aligned
- And joyful

That felt good doing that.

I am going to do my power centre mediation now.

Day 24

Not sure about the bank, maybe $65

My wages will not come in until next week I found out. I had to check and see what was happening with my teaching wages. I was expecting them and there seems to have been a miscommunication with bank numbers. I sorted that out yesterday.

I was not in the mood to chat yesterday evening. I was hiding instead. I am very good at hiding as I have been doing it most of my life.

I am still feeling a bit frustrated, not sure why. I think having a run and some exercise will be a good idea. I just feel agitation in my body.

I have been telling everyone else how important it is to put down a healthy template in their life, so it is good for me to practice what I preach. I tell people to eat healthy, get outside in nature, take action to feel better and get moving.

Best I take my own advice, which I am. This diary is part of me taking action.

I was reading about earth releasing or recycling as a way of releasing and dealing with chi, prana or energy. I will just release a little agitation, even though there is a cat sitting on me now and she is pawing at my hands and doing the cat diggy clawing thing.

It is good to consciously let go and there are many, many ways to do this. I will choose one of those now.

......

I let go of some frustration and I smiled at my heart and saw my heart smiling back.

I feel like I need to run and have some exercise and let some more energy go. Drumming can also do this, though not this early in the morning and while I have guests downstairs.

What can I manifest with feeling today?

I am going to manifest how feels having more financial freedom.

I know I can go shopping for whatever because I have financial freedom to choose.

It feels amazing feeling the freedom.

I can pay my bills easily and I do not have to be concerned about the when or the why. As soon as the bills come in I get my book keeper to pay them as that is what she does best. I can choose to buy what I want when I want and especially for the teenagers and they like that.

Things are working out for me. I feel a spark is ignited in me and I am letting the spark shine.

I am illuminated, I can feel the golden light rays illuminating me and feel them radiating out.

All is well and my money is working for me and not the other way round. I get my reality working for me, this is how it will be, this is how it is.

10.48 P.M.

Woo Hoo Money arrived in my account, plus I have earned $300 from clients

This morning I did a mantra whilst running and it was great. I was visualising my light and abundance radiating out and it drawing the same back into my life.

I felt really good having a run and doing this at the same time. Even my aching knee feels better today. It is definitely well worth my while to keeping running, as it is making me feel good and that is really what matters. I have enjoyed it.

I was told I am obsessed today and maybe I am. I have worked so hard all my life and yer I know I am a workaholic and when I think of my past life experiences being a work addict is hugely preferable to other addictions. I am not sure about how I feeling about others putting me down like that.

I wanted to master the art of being successful business woman and today I really felt like one. Clients are now coming and going, plus I had an interview online, which was excellent. It was a great experience and I laughed and laughed.

I know that feeling good is important.

This morning I was reminiscing about twenty four days ago. I really did feel in a shit space in the beginning of this journey. I was really sick of living like I was. I feel like things are all coming together for me and life is great.

I am going to go over the past information about the seventeen blocks to success. I had a list of the blocks to a successful business and when I first looked at this list I had six blocks. This is like having seventeen locks on your door to success and whether it is one or six locks that are locked. You cannot open the door and walk through when there is just one lock keeping it shut.

I know I have educated myself, learnt mew systems and have dealt with the majority of these blocks.

Knowing my message was one of these blocks has been priceless. This has changed over the last few weeks as I have more focus with my message now.

I look forward to my business working for me and not the other way round. I am looking at the big picture of my desired future.

I know I have the content and the packages, I have the IP, the knowledge, the expertise and the models and the processes. I want to have the leads now. Once I have enough leads then the entire business becomes self-sustaining and the practise and business will move and grow.

I have been working in a local clinic as a practitioner there. I still have not had many clients there so I am not feeling the groove being there. I will see where it leads in the future.

I think it is time to share some good vibes.

Gratitude is always good.

Today I appreciated having four clients because it shows me what I want and how easy it can be.

I also appreciated my run, it was good and I felt good being able to run further and further.

I also appreciate learning I have to let things go that make me unhappy because I know I am making myself feel stressed and angry over it all. I will focus on me and what I am doing, as well as what makes me happy.

That is of paramount importance.

Day 25

The dog is trying to cough and vomit on the floor, lovely.

I had a bit of a breakdown this morning and was quite broken for a while.

I still have a headache because of it all.

I felt like I had an amalgamation of all the rage, injustices, wrong doings and stuff that I have experienced in my life and it sort of came together and was cutting me in half. I have a colourful history of abuse on all levels and every now and then it can rise to the surface as I am obviously ready to let more go.

I took these feelings out of my body, all the rage and the hate I had been harbouring in my body. I was sitting in it and being present with what was happening, which was a breakthrough. We have to welcome the shit and feel it to help us to release it.

Not sure if that makes sense.

I could see and connect with my wounded child who was feeling alone, lost vulnerable, hidden, scared and I felt it all coming up and out of my body. It was quite amazing in hindsight, though it did feel raw and real at the time.

I feel quite exhausted now.

I spent from 10am to 3pm and finished my emails, applying

for jobs for my partner, clearing out emails and listening to some information about getting leads coming to me.

The information was about using the power of videos for leads.

It does seem that making videos is a good thing to do. There is so much info out there about "how to make your business successful'. People always have their way to do this and there are so many programs and courses it can get overwhelming ad confusing knowing what is a right fit.

Thinking about it I believe it is really about how you feel with what you are doing that is vital.

This means it does not have to be about the 'how' we do things to drive our business. It is about how we feel and how aligned and happy we are when we do these things because this shows and others pick up on it.

If you think about it we can see when someone is confident or not. We can surely consciously and subconsciously see when someone is being authentic or not.

This woman I was listening to was talking about looking for the reasons as to why and what is the reason I want success in my business. I will explore that.

Why do I want my business to be successful?

I want my children to be proud of me.

I believe I have fear and desire about wanting to succeed. Let me explore.

What do I fear?

- Failing
- Having wasted my time
- Disappointing my family
- Disappointing myself
- Not feeling good enough
- Losing my home

I do not really want to focus on these things, though if I explore the fear I can also explore the desire.

What is it that I desire?

- My kids to be proud of me
- For my eldest son to see I have made wise choices - he seems to be the hardest to please when it comes to business choices
- I want a travelling lifestyle
- I want to publish my books
- I want freedom and choices
- To take my kids away when I want
- To be financially secure for my future
- I want a better quality of life
- I want to touch and help to change people's lives
- I want to be happy and free
- I want to go where I want, when I want

So the question I now want to ask myself is
"What do I do and what would I like to earn?"
$60,000 would be a great start.

If I divide this by twelve months, then this means I have to earn $5,000 a month.

This then comes $1,153 a week and $166 a day.

If I do this then that means that this has to be $230 for 5 days of the week.

So the bottom line is I need one and a half clients a day.

This gives me a good target.

If I want one and a half clients five days a week, then I would have to make twelve sales calls to do this. Over five days that would be sixty calls a week.

This would be a great SMART goal and I will write it up after I have buffered my posts.

Day 26

Not sure of bank balance, not checked.

Today I went to a Law of Attraction Meetup and it was entertaining. I feel better after that.

I am in a better feeling space today.

I just put a post out about 'What do you do to raise your vibration?'

Meditation and mindfulness was one reply.

It is good to know what others do to make themselves feel good. There does seem to be common themes for us all.

I raise my vibration with music, dancing, singing, art and being surrounded by nice people.

I am becoming very mindful of the people that I surround myself with.

Positive, supportive happy, respectful and loving people are the best. I want more of these people in my life please universe.

Day 27

I have been thinking more about what I do when I want to raise my vibration and I want to expand my list.

- Drumming
- Smiling at others
- Uplifting music
- Exercising
- Swimming in the warm sea
- Meditating
- Listening to uplifting people
- Laughing in great company
- Watching comedy
- Having a sleep or a nanna nap
- Singing
- Dancing
- Being creative
- Reading a positive book
- Patting or cuddling the dog or cat
- Having a hug or cuddle
- Great sex

- Telling or listening to jokes
- Sending or receiving love, …..

I am sure I can think of more things now I have started to be open to it.

10.15 A.M.

I am at a course for the next two and a half days, so I will be here and there and I will write when I can.

I have asked myself a question to find out what blocks there are that I have, that stop me from truly stepping into my radiance as I see myself floundering now and then.

I am looking forward to unveiling that blockage and fear and to allow myself to radiate and shine.

I am aware of my fears of success and also about the fact that I do not want to do this journey alone. I would love to share it with someone who I can trust and share this journey with regards to anything that I do.

I look forward to having a loving and supportive partner who says things like "Go get em." And "You have got this babe."

I have worked joint ventures with many people in the past, though none of these ventures have really ever come to any fruition.

Now I feel like I do not want to walk my journey alone. I would love to have a team who are on the same page as me and who are as passionate about changing lives and lifting global consciousness as much as I am.

Maybe it is time for me to accept my feelings of being alone, so I can move past that.

This could well be a possibility and be a block that stops me connecting with likeminded people.

I know action is best being taken from the good feeling space and re-reading what I wrote tells me I am not in this space today.

What divine action can I take to get myself in that space?

I could sleep, read, meditate, walk in nature or even listen to some uplifting music.

The real question is "Will I do that?'

Day 28

I had a huge sleep.

I am not sure where my bank balances are or whether that is truly an indication of where I am or not. Who knows?

Anyway.........

I had some interesting dreams about the fact that I was living in a space where there were two realities and I was walking between both spaces at the same time.

In the two worlds we existed in both worlds at the same time. When one was closed down the other one lived and shone and visa versa. It was like the ideal thing was to have balance in both worlds. I woke up feeling all excited. It was quite interesting.

I am now in my business head.

I am good and feeling much more confident with what is happening and now I know that the most important thing for me is to feel good.

This is what matters most.

So what is working for me?

Positive self-talk, sharing and feeling gratitude, listing things that inspire me, letting go of unresolved emotions that are not serving me, allowing my greatness to shine, being happy, having visions of my future and how I want it to be, doing things that make me laugh and feel good.

All these things are working fabulously for me, what has to happen now is I have to stay disciplined and to keep doing these things active and happening regularly and consistently. This is very important as I have to let momentum grow, build and stay.

What feels good for you?

People have commented on my livestreams and have given me some great feedback. It is good for me to keep doing them, as long as they feel good.

It is time to let go of the resistance and to keep moving forward.

Plus.…. It is time to get dressed and keep re-affirming myself.

7.40 A.M.

What can I be grateful for?

I am grateful for good friends.

I am grateful for the connections I have made with others.

I am grateful learning about myself. Yesterday I was learning about aspects of my ego that can lead me to judge myself and others.

This man was talking about the four aspects of the ego that do not serve us. These are righteousness, entitlement, neediness and victimhood. I sat and pondered to see if I could be authentic about any of these behaviours, after all I cannot release them until I acknowledge them.

I was aware that I can be righteous and superior to others. I am also aware that I want to walk in and help heal others, even when they have not come to me and asked. This could be neediness and wanting to be needed even when others have not asked.

This is a good observation as it means I am caretaking others and this then stops them sorting out their own stuff and it distracted me from my path.

I have wanted to help push people into the light. It is like I am pushing them there because I see what people want and need and I know how simple and easy it will be for them to just do A or B. This does not work in reality as people have to be ready to change and move on.

This is my gift to know what will help to make others flourish, though first it is important for me to flourish first and foremost before I help others. It has to be me first.

I was aware that I have been judging people and am being critical of their approach because I see that is it not serving them. This of course is denying them their journey, which really is nothing to do with me. People have to learn in thir own way and time.

Why do I need to get involved in others' lives?

I am aware of my righteousness, my judgments, my needs and my entitlement.

Now I am aware of these things I can pick myself up on it. When I am having a conversation with someone and I feel the need to be right or to be heard, I can be aware that I am doing that and if possible stop myself before I do it.

I can change this pattern.

Yesterday I was learning about the art of facilitation and being able to hold space easily, when other things are happening to me. This is the value of being secure and grounded.

This is a great tool too.

I would like to keep clearing any energy out of my body that is not serving my highest and greatest good.

I will do a meditation and focus on clearing any jealousy, criticism, judgement, entitlement, superiority, righteousness and victimhood from my body right now.

8.15 A.M.

I have just cleared some energy and I want to share.

Where or what in my body was I harbouring energy?

- Criticism – in my head
- Judgement – silver
- Entitlement – band on my head
- Superiority – head
- Righteousness – chest
- Victimhood – all my body
- Neediness – in my lungs

Day 29

Sort of not sure about the bank

Checking my bank balance is sort of feeling insignificant now as things have changed and I am in a different space. Looking at my bank balance is counting numbers. Focusing on how I am feeling is becoming far more important.

I believe when I started this diary I was in a very needy space, now I do feel totally different.

I feel that when I am aligned and feeling good, then things line up for me and I know that money comes in.

This is a great awareness.

I know now the most important thing for me to do is to feel good and feel my radiance shine.

I believe I do not need to be a millionaire and go and buy an island any more, I want to merely enjoy life.

I want a great quality of life which enables me to be to be able to have more freedom and choice in my life. I love to travel and go when and where I want to. I am seeing value in other things more than before.

This is great as it has taken my focus and value away from money and more to my quality and better things in life. Before this it was about the money, now it is about the lifestyle.

I see value in quality time, great friends, community, happy activities, and basically enjoying life.

I am still at my workshop. I am at the end of my twelve month commitment to this business mastery course I made to myself and it is interesting to see who is still standing here at the end.

There have been quite a few girls who have dropped out. I am still here, still turning up and still doing the work, which is worth commending within itself.

I had another realisation yesterday. Writing always helps for me to have realisations. This realisation I had was that I really have everything that I need. It is all right here ad right now.

My journey now is about applying it and knowing that I am enough, just as I am.

The course carries on tomorrow and I will go home tonight after work, because it feels good for me right now. That is enough. All I have to do is to do the feel good thing.

Plans have been made, direction given, message understood and it's time to CEE ME just as I am.

Connect, earth and educate is my thing.

I have to make the phone calls.

I have to bring the motivation in and the desire to do that. I will see myself connecting with people and enjoying the connection.

I know I can bring in that energy, so I will.

I want to be in a place to work with people that I like, doing what I love and it feeling more like living my dream rather than going to work.

Things are always working out for me.

Day thirty one will be a thirty day commitment to make the connections, twenty connections a week would be great.

I love making the calls. I know the rewards that I have to give in CEEing other people happy.

I am valued and my value extends out for all to see. I radiate light and I have planted the seeds for the next 18 years.

I want happiness, fun, laughter, freedom, choice, genuineness, integrity, and radiance.

My connections are positive, happy and polite.

I am grounded enough in who I am.

I honour and know people do what they do, it is their journey and that is fine.

Everything is all fine.

Day 30

It is time for action today.

I will look at what I need to do to get the peeps knocking at my door.

I know I have lots to offer and that is great because people come to see and learn more. They love doing the activities recommended by me.

I have so much knowledge and information to offer that is extremely useful and I have lots to educate and teach about.

I appreciate my life.

I am a self-sustaining spiritual human who is on my journey.

I think I will go and ground myself and then it will be time for a run.

I am feeling a bit scattered and it's time to centre myself.

Day 31

Today is day one of making the phone calls.

It's letting people know when and how they can work with me. It's reaching out to new people and bringing in that confidence to do that.

Yesterday I did two lots of one hundred positive statements and I have two new client enquiries, with one new client today.

I spent most of yesterday sorting out paperwork and tying up loose ends.

I have to keep videoing and doing my thing. I can see where that is going and where that is taking me.

I can see what it is that I have to do now to get fresh people and leads into my life. I will keep finding ways for that to happen. All is well and things are always working out for me.

I am going to dream of my Personal Assistant (PA).

I love having an assistant. She is great!

That pile of stuff I had piled up is almost done and she enjoyed doing these jobs. She is great at selling me and is always so polite and happy and the customers just love her. It works a treat.

I love being around her.

I like the fact that she always want to know more and is happy to explore more ways to benefit us all. I love that about her.

I also love the fact that she has these great ideas and the way that she approaches me with them is great.

She will say "what if we ….." Then I know she is going to come out with one of her good ideas.

Once we decide on the next plan of action, she gives me a new 'To do' list.

She says "I see if you are able to …… then I can …."

I can see where she is heading with these ideas.

She asks me to write copy for this and that, so off I go. Then she says what if again and we edit the changes. Her style is great.

She knows that things are working out for us both.

She has a very keen eye and she sees an 'A' grade client when there is one.

This works for us all, as not only does she get paid, she also earns great commission.

She knows this initial work load will pay off for all of us and that over time things are going to get easier for us both as things become more automated and templated.

Putting the energy in now brings lots of passive income later.

I love being in her presence when she is here, though she does also work from home as well.

I feel lots of comfort and security working with her and she feels the same.

I am off to have a run and shout out my manifestations.

It is time to shout and run out loud.

Day 32

I made those phone calls yesterday which were great.

It was a good start.

I even got a client doing it, just by picking up the phone. More manifesting like that would be fabulous.

I was going over some stuff yesterday and I realised that I have come a long way in twelve months and I have certainly learnt a lot. I look forward to seeing what is going to happen in the next twelve months.

Having more of an online presence would be good.

I am grateful for yesterday.

I am grateful for seeing the big picture. I am grateful for the opportunities I have coming up in my life. I am grateful for my experiences because I like the variety of those in my life. I am grateful for my clients because it is easy. I appreciate easy ways of earning a living because it gives me time to do what I want to do which is paint, sing, dance, and create.

I am about to paint my first Bob Ross painting at the moment.

I like painting. I hope I can read my writing when it comes time to type this up.

I will be proud of my first landscape painting.

Yesterday I said two rounds of one hundred statements. I am committed.

I always do these out loud and fast, usually whilst walking on the beach. It does not take very long.

I said 'As my radiance grows, my abundance glows' or I get it mixed up 'As my radiance glows, my abundance grows.' Either way it does not matter as it is all growing and glowing.

I like this one, it feels good and I can feel my energy rising and getting myself getting pumped up.

I also like the 'I am valued and I give value' as well. Just keeping saying them and talking them up creates a shift of energy, it literally takes 10 minutes.

Today I will set some dates and will call some venues for prices. I will do that this morning after my painting.

I am going off walking now and I am looking forward to painting.

Day 33

Not sure what to write, I have a mental blank.

My eldest son had his Deb ball last night. It was a good night, I had a few wines and possibly embarrassed him though that is in my job description as that is just the type of mum that I am. I was not too embarrassing. I was just being an open loving mum.

I was very proud of him and I didn't even cry. How good was that?

After drinking I wanted a cigarette though I did not, I am very pleased with myself and I am grateful for that.

Yesterday I made some more phone calls and sent some emails out about public speaking, which was also great.

I will endeavour to keep following that path as I know speaking gigs are great for me. I love it, it gives me a great buzz and it works so well.

I was also grateful yesterday for something that I will not repeat here, that is my personal life and I am here about my business life, so let's stay in the business mind.

1. I am grateful and happy that I pushed through a barrier and I have started making some phone calls.

2. I am happy and grateful that I appreciate the ease of doing another plant Thymes newsletter and putting it out there.

3. I am happy and grateful that I appreciate my ability to follow through even when I wanted to pike out. Now I see the benefit of connecting with others and giving them value in their lives, they then return this value to me.

Day 34

Cold, it's a bloody cold day today.

It's all so cold, I just want to go outside and lie in the sun.

I appreciated having a bath in my bathroom now because I was so cold, I got in it. It really helped me to warm up. I was freezing before.

I washed the dog and did not do much else.

I spent a little time researching Shakti pat and seeing what or how it could be done. That probably makes no sense. I am still working it out myself. My understanding is that is a process, primarily in India, where they release unwanted energies and entities. I am quite intrigued by it.

I also wanted to find a way to take on the energy of someone who is my model. This is modelling others.

It is like seeing the good traits in others and then bringing that energy into your own life. This is not in a way that you are taking from them. It is a way of bringing good energy into your life, such as confidence, motivation and excitement.

It was here that I came across the ancient practise of Shakti pat. This is a practise that appears to be practised and still is in India. It was interesting to watch.

I would like to Shakti pat the organisational skills of my mentor and take on some of her vibes, the good ones that will help and serve me for my highest and greatest good.

8.30 P.M.

It has been a relaxing day today.

I did a template for a sales page and a launch page for freebie give away and I now know how to create the landing pages. I just have to get on with it.

It's still raining here. In fact it's been raining all day. It is so dam cold here, Brrrrr.

I know that the cold does close and shut me down.

Onwards and upwards my friends. I will give some gratitude today.

I am grateful for getting more clients in the door.

I am grateful for having dinner cooked for me.

I am grateful for a hot bath which helped me to warm up and I am grateful for feeling good.

Day 35

Bank details have been up and down, though no longer feeling the need to look at it any more. I was able to acknowledge where I was in the beginning and that has been done now and I will move on.

I do not want to focus on the numbers. I want to focus on the good feelings.

I have been on the beach again saying my mantra. I said my two regular mantras one hundred times each. I like doing this. I really feel it raising my vibration.

I spoke with seven clients, two became paying clients and four were potential and one will come today. Woo Hoo.

Someone is also interested in doing my eight week coaching program, which is great.

I have another client tomorrow and maybe one or two later in the week, which is fabulous.

I appreciate my busy day with clients. It was good and I managed to do and get a few things done that I have not been able to do for a while.

I appreciate being busy and people seeing the value that I have to give. I appreciate people coming to me and wanting to learn and share about my expertise.

I appreciate my interview videos that my friend sent to me, she cut and edited them and they look great. There is a great intro video and I love it.

I love that and I believe that things are looking up. In fact I know that things are looking up from here on it.

I will play the ten clients a week game as that is working for me.

I am busy which is excellent. I now have decided that will have a clearer and cleaner focus on my income. This saves me lots of time and energy in my life.

I arrange my clients now on my chosen work days Mondays, Tuesdays morning and on Thursdays work best for me.

I book one or two clients on Tuesday mornings and four to five on Monday and Thursdays.

I have time for me and I schedule some 'Me' time in my week. This is extremely vital in my busy business life. I have regular bodywork and pampering, after all I have the money and I can afford it. This makes me feel excited and is important for me to honour myself.

I love the interactions I have with people. I have discovered that I have a regular model in place which works for me. If I know if I keep this up I will put up my prices to $660 per session, which is a great idea, I look forward to that.

I know things are working out for me now.

Good for me.

Goodnight.

Day 36

Some days I get slack with my diary, which is me getting slack in my desire to manifest my future.

That's okay though. We all have up and down days and I am looking forward to less depths of the up and downs and to have longer extended periods of joyous and happy days.

I made $150 this morning. Things are looking up and clients are coming in. I really appreciate this.

I did not do any mantras this morning as I walked with someone on the beach this morning and they were chatting away, as it was their birthday.

I am on the train right now heading to the big smoke, off teaching. I will do some manifestations for my herb business.

I love selling my herbs, I love the fact that people are feeling better taking my herbs, it's great to see people glowing with good health and vitality.

People say things like "My heart burn is going down and I have gone off my medication now after 18 years."

They share their good news on Instagram and social media, this is worthy of sharing.

The herbs are easy. I have marketing campaigns constantly

running and they pick up new clientele who love to chat and connect with me.

It's more than just a chat. We love to educate our clientele to help and support them, as well as make them feel happy and have a laugh. I love to help them learn more about wondrous benefits of herbs and so do my staff.

What I love about the herbs is their energy.

They are happy herbs and they are safe, they smell good. They love being handled and shared, they are friendly, they help people to feel better, they love being of service, they give to mother nature, they come from mother nature and they know exactly what to do.

They love to heal. And they are masters of healing.

They are chemical free, additive free, easy and have their own characteristics, personality traits and happiness scales. They are happy go lucky beings who love to share the love.

They love being happy and healthy and they want that for mankind and the planet.

Things have got so busy with the herbs I have had to expand my premises and go through the accredited food handling thing which is all fine and dandy, as I know what and how to do that having done it many times before.

Back to the train journey.

Today I will try something else on my train journey. I will check out when it is necessary to see if the train continues on and if I can get off at a closer stop. I currently stop and then have to catch a tram. I have plenty of time which is great to check out a new route.

Feeling a bit sleepy now and I could easily have a nap. The gentle rocking motion of the train and the gentle clitter clatter of the rails on the tracks is soothing to my soul.

I was listening to something today about living with the polarity of life.

We have two ends of the pole. I know that and teach that already. Let's use the example of being rich or poor. I commonly see this as a stick which has the two ends. One end is rich and one end is poor. This is the polarity of life with each end of the stick being either end of the pole.

This person was looking at this as a triangle or a funnel. On the one side is great wealth and the other side is great poverty.

From here we can explore the extremeness of both sides.

When, where, how, with whom, why, does it serve me?
How would it be if I was one or the other of those sides?
What would I feel and why would I want that?
Would I react differently to situations in my life?
I am so great at exploring new concepts.

If I explore both sides of the funnel unpack it, I will increase awareness to it and as our awareness increases our funnel opens up more and more. This is a nice concept to visualise, especially for a visual person like me.

Limiting thoughts lead to limiting outcomes.

Therefore a good aim for me would be to see myself open to allow more people, types of clientele, opportunities and abundance to come in from that side of the funnel or triangle. I have experienced one side for some time now. I am ready to balance this funnel out.

I open my funnel to more abundance.

I allow and let abundance come in.

Day 37

Day 38

I missed a day.

I was moving well with my motivation and then I fell prey to an ulcer on the bottom of my tongue that came up in a couple of hours.

I was not able to eat yesterday until about 2 p.mm ish and that was after I had put golden thread (which is a herb) on it.

Today it is still here, though my tongue is not as swollen. It is right at the back of my mouth and the pain sort of stopped me drinking and eating, swallowing and even speaking.

That would not have stopped me writing. I was not in the mood to be honest.

I will check out what the tongue means now.

Tongue is about the ability to taste the pleasure of life with joy.

Ulcers are fear or a strong belief that I am not good enough and this is eating away at me.

This means I still have fear. More energy to clear.

I have not booked my workshop dates because I believe there is a fear of failure or not getting in the numbers. I have not even given it a go.

I am avoiding that which potentially can alright I suppose and

139

I am not in a space where I am willing to take risks. It is not a feel good flow I am having about it at the moment.

I was learning about FB Business manager and the potential of using it to do an online business.

I could put courses, products, in fact all my stuff on there.

It does mean that I have to spend time to learn something new. Learn a new program, a new process and a new way of doing something. I would have to install it, sort it, create it, sort key words, update info, and the list goes on.

It will take time to get it happening and the question is do I want to learn another new thing?

I am not sure if I am up to learning a whole new program that could still not guarantee business. It sort of feels like I am chasing that shiny object again.

I will move onto something else.

I mixed up some of my herbs that I have downstairs in my dispensary and I made a herbal mix for me.

I was feeling a little flat and know my nutrient levels are getting low. Even eating a healthy diet we can all lack nutrients in our diet as our food is so processed.

When I take my herbs it helps the tide to turn inside and I start to feel more energised and alert. It is good for me to take my own herb products to.

This will get my nutrient levels up. I soon pep up once I start to take any of my super green mixes.

My current body ailments are on my feminine side of my body. I am annoyed about my partner and the way he treats his body which indicates I have the issue with how I am treating my body.

I always know that when someone pisses me off, I have shit to sort. I would be good for me to change how I treat my body. All of that is easily seen, felt and acknowledged.

I know I am feeling agitated. We do not have much time really connecting together. There is so much time talking about 'other' things, doing things and not being things. I can feel unheard and invalidated.

I have to go and buy a birthday present today.

I had another meditate a little while ago. My higher self is telling me to chill and take it easy. It tells me to stop pushing myself so hard.

My vision and my meditation went back to my father leaving me at three or four and I was feeling fear and frustration.

What is also quite interesting is my ulcer came up within 12 hours of me being told that my father believes I was not a 'Plant' and neither are my children. This comment was Chinese whispers said to me, from he said and she said.

Whether it was gossip or not, it still gave me was a feeling of being insignificant, again. I am a bit over this coming up in my life.

This has happened again and again.

I told my mother that she can say something to him about this or else I will.

I feel it would be good for me to express how I truly feel.

I have done this in the past and I have never received any acknowledgement. Santa Claus is never coming.

Day 39

Not sure of bank, no longer checking, not important, don't care. I had a client yesterday that spent $650.

This was excellent, hair analysis, healing, herbs and he also booked future healing sessions. I have worked with this guy about five years ago, so it was interesting him coming back.

I said to him a long time ago that you need to sort your physical health out. I gave him a Louise warning and he did not heed my advice. Now he is quite sick.

This was great. I have bills to pay and I can pay them all now. Woo Hoo.

So I will give some appreciations.

Dear Universe

I appreciate my tongue healing and being able to swallow and to feel pain free.

I appreciate my clients coming to do the workshop and for healing session.

I appreciate my body healing itself and knowing exactly what to do every time. I believe this is fabulous and truly a miracle. There really is nothing I have to do, as my body knows what it innately needs and wants.

Yesterday I learnt that the reason most people do not succeed is because of their beliefs and the most common belief that people have is

"I don't deserve to have lots of money".

The antidote to this belief is,

"I deserve to be successful and wealthy, I value myself and I am worthy of wealth."

I am going to walk the dogs and I will repeat this statement as many times as I see fit.

9.30 P.M.

My bank balance got up to $890, woo hoo

I know I am not counting anymore, though I had to have a boast.

I appreciate people coming to me.

I feel the Chi (energy) growing and my radiance growing. I know things are always working out for me, which is fabulous.

I appreciate the big bag of dog biscuits, filling up the chicken bin full of chicken food, paying off my debts and being done with them. These are great ways to appreciate what is happening for me.

Let's explore the fact that I am doing great things in my business and the business is pumping now and money is coming in.

As my business pumps I am grateful for being able to help others and to help a wider range of people.

I am open to looking for ways to help others.

I buy some land in a remote unindustrialised place, in some poor area of the world. Poor in this example is in a sense of dollars and cents. Not poor in their quality of life.

In this place I grow organic veggies and I teach the locals how to do this. I show them how they can support themselves financially by growing a beautiful food that benefits the health of them and their families.

Part of this journey would be for me to pay locals and to teach them how to use their time and energy to be able to grow this organic food for orphanages. To help feed children healthy vital food, especially to the young whose bones and bodies are growing and if they are given healthy and nutritious food, they will be healthier and happier.

I could even create a foundation to help others donate money to help them to do similar projects or things to empower and change others lives. I also give training and education to abused men and woman. These ideas here are limitless.

I pay someone with a high sense of morals and knowledge who will be there to help others and who have a similar vision. They love to help people to empower other women and children to feel safe and confident.

We teach them tools like martial arts, spiritual practices, self-care practises and help to give them the tools and support that will help them to empower and drive their own lives.

I offer education to children that need it.

It would be excellent to create my own Hogwarts School for magic and for the gifted.

That would work very well for me and for others to.

Day 40

Ok, its day 40.

I am out in the bush at someone's half built house.

There is so much I could do with this house and there is so much that needs to be done in this place.

Ok so what am I going to write about today?

I am going to write about the house I am going to buy on an island. I heard today there are cheap homes in Hamilton Island and I got excited thinking about it.

It is a home I want to buy and not a house. I know the difference between a home and a house. I would love to have a beautiful home.

I write, create and paint in my beautiful setting.

I enjoy island life. My partner is doing that they love to do, whether being creative, building something, exercising, meditating, sailing, fishing, all the things that they love to do.

I have been chatting with my children and talking about when I buy my block of land and get back off the grid. I tell them how great it is going to be.

I would love to have at least twenty acres.

The kids will have their own motorbikes or four-wheelers.

I have horses, chooks, goats and some Damara sheep. That

would be good. The sheep can have acres acres and the rest of us have the rest.

I have a big veggie patch with organic home grown yummy vegetables.

On the farm I build a rammed earth home which would not be square. It would have wiggly walls that would be very wiggly. I would have tepees for WWoofers and for B and B people.

We have lots of space and fun, which is great.

We grow our own food, make our own wine and grow lots of herbs and spices, as well as fruits and nuts.

It is so great being back off the grid and on the land.

There is no mains power, instead I have dams, bores, rain water, solar and wind power, compost toilet and recyclable great water systems.

Just the way I like it to be.

Day 41

I had to get up twice to pee last night. That was a bit annoying. The cold does not help.

I was also having some strange dreams of clearing up halls and blocks of land, as well as finding Greek people's wallets that were full of cash. What fabulous dreams.

I was also growing hazelnuts and other nuts. I was going all over everything. I was cleaning things, picking up things and sorting things out. It certainly was a busy dream. Anyway I am glad it's all over, even though it was just a dream.

It is Sunday morning today.

I have a client today which is good for my purse, though not for the fact it is on a Sunday. I am also targeting people to get them into my workshop in September. I have one in and another one ready to come. I also have a few leads to follow up and see how they are faring.

Onwards and upwards.

It is time to take my herbs, drink some water and go for a walk.

This week I did not book my workshops, not sure why I am still procrastinating. I also did not make any enquiries about any public speaking gigs. That is not helping me to move forward. I will have to see about that and what it is that is stopping me.

It is time for Earth Church.

I asked myself "Why is it that I am sitting here, is it divine timing or what is it?"

I got inspiration from a book saying

"Stop avoiding stepping out into my power, It is time to be powerful and radiant."

I like that and I will do just that.

That is what I want.

10.20 P.M.

Not a busy day.

I had my client and that was good. I have decided I will use this time to put out a request to the universe for people for my workshop.

It is time to see it pumping.

I am not feeling the 'pump' so I will see that value that people get.

I see the value in people owning up to their own stuff.

I know the value to be had when people learn to connect to their bodies and for then to feel freer and at home in their own bodies.

I know as people clear their shit they feel better.

I know the joy and freedom we can have when we release and let go of stuff.

I also know the freedom that we can have as the truth always sets us free.

I know that the happiness to be had by looking inside at what is going on and to give yourself a sense of freedom from that.

I know the power of love.

I know the power of awareness and validation.

I know the power of connection and I know and have seen the changes that happen to people when they work with me.

I like seeing people happy.

I love seeing families coming together.

I love seeing the light bulb moment that comes inside others when they have awareness as to how they have been living their lives and when they know where they have to go to find freedom.

Day 42

Been an on and off day.

I am still getting clients coming in.

I checked on my clinic day and I had a client booked in, lucky that I checked. I have been so busy and I just presumed I had no-one booked in, so now I am busier, I will have to check regularly.

I still have not got round to finishing my landing page and sales page. I have been distracting myself with other things and my personal life.

I am very aware of the fact that any upsets in my personal life impinges on my ability to radiate and shine wealth.

I went to the dentist this morning and my tooth is a bit sore now. I had two fillings, one was quite big. This is a good thing.

I know I needed to go and before I was not able to afford it.

It was just another thing that got put out on the back burner. So I am glad I am able to do this and I appreciate having happy teeth. My tooth is aching now though.

As I was sitting on this chair with half of my face numb I am telling myself I am worthy of being able to able to honour and respect my body.

It is important to acknowledge the value of my body, as they say, "My body is a temple."

I am worthy of this. I am worthy of looking after my teeth and I value my teeth.

The dentist did say I ideally would have been better for me to have had come and visit her sooner and I actually got a bit teary when I was saying that I could not afford it. I choose to see this as a good thing.

I did have a win. I have three people booked into my workshop, which is excellent. Thanks Universe.

One person just booked out of the blue and I am excited about that. I never had that before and they just paid on Paypal, easy. I love easy. I love it when money comes in easily for me.

There was no need for chasing anything, so I am going to appreciate some stuff before my pen runs out.

- I appreciate having the money to look after my teeth
- I appreciate having a booking just out of the blue
- I appreciate the fact that it is easy
- I appreciate adapting to ease
- I appreciate it when things are working out for me
- Thanks Universe, I appreciate you

Day 43

It is still bloody cold here.

Not sure when spring is going to arrive.

Been feeling 'slumpy', it is the best way to describe it.

I feel like something is coming and I am sort of in the middle of it.

I spent yesterday creating landing pages and trying to sort lagging videos and then I lost all my accounts data\base on my book keeping program. That proved to be interesting.

The day ended up being quite frustrating.

So today I am going for a walk down the beach. I will chat later.

I am on the train to the city, going back to teaching again.

I am curious as to what changes there are happening within me.

I realised that fun is not something that I have had a lot of in my life and I have been asking for more of it. I am wondering if I know what it is, as it has been forgotten for so long.

I have seen and witnessed and reflected on the days that I sit in my power and I radiate out my presence and I honour my value and my worth, then I find I get value back.

It is definitely noticeable now, so much so that I know that the

152

most important thing for me to do is to stay centred and happy and then to stay as such.

I have moved from 'Oh my god, I have no money and life is shit' to 'There is always more value that I can have.' I see that as I acknowledge my value so much more now. It does reflect in my outside world.

I had two herb orders come in over the past forty-eight hours and I asked twice for this. I will ask again right here and now.

Universe please send me another herb order, another easy order would be great.

I created an Instagram page for the herbs and have to post and share it about now. I know that consistency is of vital importance here. Slowly, slowly is the game here.

I see that changes in beliefs can take time. I see the effects of daily disciplined practise and how that has its effect.

My youngest son asked me for something this week and I was aware that I said "Sure." I did not even have to check my bank or anything like that. I just made the arrangements and bought what he wanted. It all just flowed well. I even made the point of saying to him, "Sure thing buddy, money is coming in for us now." It is good that we are earning and working now and that we are in a more financially secure position. I appreciate that. I have even been learning about sacred abundance, which is great and very interesting.

I am feeling ready to take the leap and to jump into the next phase of moving forward and to keep making changes.

I will keep on focusing on what is happening for me and I will not stop there. I will continue daily practices.

- Affirmations
- Mantras
- Writing things one hundred times
- Saying things over and over.

I have not written the one hundred times words here, as that would be very boring for everyone to read. You can try it for yourself.

It is a great exercise to do and it works very well and very quickly. Give it a go. All that you are basically doing is rewiring your brain. It makes new neural pathways and wraps the myelin sheaths and every time you say the statement, more myelin sheath is wrapped making more secure and solid neural connections.

It means the more you do it, the more you believe it.

I also decided I have to stop waiting.

I want to move up to warmer climates and my son has one year left in school. I do have to wait for him to finish school to leave, though I could also reframe it and use the time for something great. It is time to stop waiting and just be okay with what is happening and with what I am doing.

I know that things are always working out for me. That is true for me.

I am so ready to doze and I want to go to bed early.

Day 44

I have started waking earlier and as the sun is coming up earlier.

I meditated for twenty minutes and I could feel the stress running out of my body as I was letting it go. Better out than in, I say.

I have been exploring heart convergence stuff which is very cool. I can feel it calming my heart.

All I do is bring my attention to my heart, see it breathing and then think of something happy and loving and I breathe that in and out. It works well.

I might even sneak off for a massage today. I would really like thirty minute neck, back and shoulder massage. I feel I deserve it.

I am feeling quite dozy so I might just doze again. Mmmm

Bit of a frustrating day, I am still trying to sort out my landing pages.

I have to link sub-domains to mailing programs and then do this and that. It is not really my expertise. Change www.subscribe to bla bla, I do not know what it is all about. It is something to outsource I think as it is beyond me and it is frustrating me and making me angry.

155

I have been fiddling around with this for a couple of weeks now and now I have to admit that is it beyond me and it is too much for me to handle and do.

I am sure I can find someone to help sort it out. I have an accountability call tomorrow with someone who might be able to help which is good.

It is highly valuable to have a mentor, someone that you can be accountable to. Someone who can see things out of the box that we are in, someone to give you suggestions, someone who is successful, and someone who is doing what you want to do.

So I know I will be able to sort this problem out tomorrow with someone who creates lots of landing pages.

I have realised that my state of mind is vital and very important and today I heard a great analogy.

We are filled with water from being babies and to the first six to seven years of our lives.

We are buckets that are filled with the beliefs, thoughts and behaviours from our surroundings. This water is all our thoughts and beliefs from those around and it is our parents, siblings and peers that help us to fill our buckets.

For us to change, like me saying my daily positive statements, it is like putting pebbles in this bucket of water.

We have to keep throwing them in, one by one until we dilute or push the old water out. It is like letting out the old beliefs and then consciously choosing what I put into that bucket.

I am doing this by being aware of how I feel and my relationships to others. I choose to consciously create the life that I want to.

This is what I am going to keep doing. I will keep adding these new belief's about what it is that I want to see happen.

New pebbles of radiating my worth and value I will add in and in return I will get rewarded with new ways of living.

Day 45

I had another crazy dream.

I dreamt I was in a tsunami. I felt scared by the power and the force of the water and the water levels started rising and consuming some of the town, though the locals did not seem perturbed by it.

I am running a workshop this weekend and I asked for six attendees and only have four bookings. I was chatting with a couple last night so I will see how that goes and what happens there.

I have decided that I will not be pushing the fact anymore and it is always best to strike when the iron is hot. I have been pushing sales for too long now and I do not like it.

I also have two work frustrations that are limiting me. I am still stuck with my landing pages and I am stuck with FB Manager which is blocking my posts and my advertising campaigns. It's hard to find someone who understands this and how this works.

Writing the landing pages is easily done and I know I can change the content easily. I am all good with that part of it. It takes time for the set up. I have asked my coach in the business program that I am in for help and hopefully she can. I will be finishing my business mastery course in a couple of months.

This week I have three paying clients so far, plus the couple that I saw yesterday and I am not sure about today. I might have a new client who was a staff member of mine when I had my cafe. Her brother was shot in a gang fight a couple of weeks away and she is in a bit of a mess. I offered her a free healing session because I know she needs it.

I thought I would start my day writing some of this stuff out and getting things out of my head. Here I am.

I want to start the day on a more positive note, so I will start sharing more gratitude.

Today I am grateful and happy that I will be having a conversation with an accountability partner who will help me.

Today I am happy and grateful that I will take time to ground and centre myself.

Today I am happy and grateful that I have the choices in front of me and each day brings me opportunities and choices.

Today I am appreciating the clients I am having and specially those who have now become regulars for me.

I appreciate paying my bills on time.

I appreciate feeling good in my life.

I feel I am not quite present and in my body.

Last night I was releasing feelings of being unsettled and frustrated. That was good and I felt better afterwards.

I know what I have to do and I know how to do it.

I feel heavy in my body which feels like I want to release the 'burden' in my body.

I will meditate before I walk and get myself into my body for a start.

I have to start somewhere.

Day 46

I have to confess, a few days have passed.

I had my seminar at the weekend and it was very good. I made the executive decision to put my diary on hold because I can.

Things have definitely changed and shifted for me. Yesterday was the day after the weekend and I was tidying things up, plus I had two clients.

I appreciate the clients and work that has been coming in. It is excellent.

My physical health went off track over the weekend, though I am back on track again now and all is well. When I am holding space, facilitating, arranging cooking and running the show, I can tend to do whatever I have to so I can get things done. I also have lots of cakes and snacks at the weekend and I tend to comfort eat.

I have learnt not focus on what I don't want and to focus on what I do want. It is a great idea and it works.

I want to get some more dates to run a seminar or two and I will find some new venues. I will make some enquiries today.

I have put it off and put it off and now it is time to do something about it.

1.45 P.M.

I am on the train to the city and I am feeling so much better, so I will keep on keeping on.

This is the work that needs to be done and this is how it's carried out and what is best happening for me.

When I mean the work to be done I mean taking the time to write and focus on how I want my life to be and doing it consistently that these new pebbles tip out the old and stale water.

Writing this journal has taught me so much about myself, my business and what I want for my future. All those things seem to have changed or are so much clearer now and this has been less than two months.

I see my future and it looks amazing.

I have a block of land that is paying for itself. In fact I am thinking of buying another property as I am now in the position to do so and I can. I have discovered that by renting them my investment property it earns us very good income and it is easy.

It is all easy. In fact it is so easy that I have decided to employ a property manager which is making my life even easier.

People like my quaint little home and they love living there. The property pays me getting $42,000 a year and I can offset my other property. There it is.

It is so easy doing this.

My financial advisor is a gem and I love his ideas and style. Being debt free is becoming a closer reality to me day by day. He understands the tax implications and it lets me understand what the wisest moves to make my money and assets work for me. I like making it easier and he explains things clearly to me so I understand.

So how will that look like?

It will be extraordinary because I have so much free time. I go away and visit the places that I want to visit. I am ticking off the places and adventures off my bucket list.

Louise's Bucket List

- Track down family history in Africa
- Visit South America
- Go on a cruise in the Caribbean
- Go to city in Burma or Nepal
- Own a muscle car again — mustang or corvette?
- Go Drag Racing
- Go Rally Driving
- Get my motorbike license
- Take the kids to Northern Territory
- Go to Cooper Pedy
- Swim with Dolphins in tropical waters
- Be farming in Bali
- Ride freely on my horses
- Visit Egypt
- Walk on the great wall of China
- Go to Grasse France when the flowers are in bloom
- Saffron Farm

I will be able to laugh and play and all will be well. That will be remarkable.

In fact I think I will be able to give up my teaching job, so there will be less driving back and forth and more free time for me. It will certainly help to embrace my creativity and fun.

I was talking with someone today about the fact that we are all taking things far too seriously. I believe that we complicate our lives and make things much harder than they need to be.

After all, how good would it be if everyone is happier and is feeling good?

I am seeing the land that I am buying as a new opportunity.

It is easy having people sharing my space and in return they love to reward me with money.

It's a win, win.

I am ready to doze now.

I will bring in some nice energy in that I will be happy and I will love my time and life.

Day 47

The days are starting to get longer and the sun is rising earlier. That's fabulous for me as I love the sun and warmth.

I came home from teaching last night and I pretty much passed out. I was so tired, maybe after my busy emotional weekend.

So what specific business discussions or manifestations can I do today?

Where will I be in 18 months?

I am living in a block of land. It will be warm and comfortable.

I have a few tepees there as farm stays. This will be a novelty for all.

The shower and the kitchen block is a renovated shed with a shower on one side and the kitchen on the other. This will make the plumbing easy and I love easy.

There will be three tepees to start, with two more coming. They will be arranged around the mess hall or the catering hall. Maybe one tepee is slightly off a little bit to give that one a little more privacy.

It looks great. The tepees are well sealed and they are bug free.

I have plenty of income coming in which is great. Things are really starting to flow now and I have a great following in my tribe.

All is well. I look forward to the next stage of my life and am already planning for my future.

10.40 P.M.

Today I believe that there are three words that I want to keep on saying more and more.

These words are

- Simple
- Easy
- and fun.

Simple, easy and fun!

Today I was a little overwhelmed with the landing pages, writing articles, as well as doing other stuff. I did notice that I was stressing out about it.

I went for a run this morning and did my positive self-talk and I was in nature which was important. It is important to mediate and possibly do my presence meditation. That always works well.

I am happy and grateful for the money in my bank.

I am happy and grateful for paying my bills easily

I am happy and grateful for people knowing and trusting my value.

I am grateful for how things are. I see the radiance shine all around me.

I love to laugh and to love to create the joy, fun and happiness that I want.

I love having fun, feeling frolicky and being in freedom.

I love feeling fun in my life.

I am happy and grateful for abundance, respect and touch in my life.

(oops I farted) He He

I continue to connect, earth and educate.

Day 48

What is it that I want today?

I want some clients to come in, I want to be selling courses, though how will people know about it, if it is not done and out there. So here goes.

This is where I will be in one months' time.

I am busy booking in clients. I have 1,000 on my mailing list.

I have six to ten clients a week. I will 'shuffle' them into my three days. Some of these clients are online and some are face to face, which is all great.

I do amazing work with my clients. They love learning with me and they love feeling better. They tell their friends about it, which I appreciate.

I love working with people who want to change, it helps me to choose new ways of helping people and learning more about them.

I know my focus is my passion and it really touches my heart when I see people shining and I see the light on their faces. I love seeing the amplifying of their energy and the lifting of their spirits and seeing them shine.

I love seeing people feeling and finding the joy within. I love seeing them feel the love and joy coming in. It feels great seeing that. It feels much better seeing their faces light up.

I love to focus on the why's and the what's of the help that I bring and have to offer.

I feel lit up when I am laughing, when I am linking to something empowering and motivating.

I feel good listening to music, when I am dancing, when I am having a laugh, I feel good when I sing, I feel good when I have direction and I know where I am going. I feel good when I am following my passion and fun.

It is simple, easy and fun for me.

9.30 P.M.

What a day!

I woke up at 5am.

I thought I had a phone call with a guy from the USA and he did not ring me.

I then had a coaching call at 6.00AM and that was great. I got two out of the four landing pages up. This is a great job done. I understand more about how I do that now.

This was a big job and I have been phucking around with it for about three weeks. I was stuck with sub domains and CNAMEs etc. Only to discover that I did not need to do any of that after all.

I got some subscribers happening already and I look forward to playing around with it more. I will do another two tomorrow and then I can see what other freebies I can put together.

Either way it is a plan that is in action.

I also plan to put together a weekend giveaway. This will be a weekend accommodation pack, I will see if it is a good way to get more email addresses.

It will be worth giving it a go. I have been putting together snippets from here and there that I have learnt over the last twelve months.

The reality will be finding my way that works for me and my business that I enjoy sharing.

I love the videos, the articles, the networking so maybe I can keep these as my focus.

Day 49

I love feeling alive and happy.

Today I woke singing "I'm alive and alert, I'm awake and joyous. I'm alive and alert, I am enthusiastic about life."

I appreciate the clients I have had and their willingness to want to change and feel good. I love knowing they are better, healthier and happier.

Yesterday I counted my YouTube videos. I have made twenty seven videos so far. I checked my views and one of them had 555 views, which is cool as I have become involved in a 555 fractal. Ha, how is that for alignment?

I appreciate clients coming out of the blue.

I appreciate the freedom I have had.

I appreciate going shopping for food because I need it.

I appreciate feeling good.

I appreciate having a laugh.

I appreciate joy and most of all I appreciate fun.

Day 50

Wow.

Ten more days to go. I can reflect on how I felt when I started this diary.

I was clutching and grabbing for money. I was struggling and counting the pennies. I was worried about where the next meal will be coming from and now all these things have changed.

Yesterday I was offered an opportunity to invest some money and I will take this opportunity and I will work with it. I feel like I am moving into a realm of sacred economy.

There are so many people who find our current money system, banking systems and our financial status as frustrating as I do. People are becoming fed up with the banks and the government departments, taxes, rules, regulations, and the bullshit that has to goes with it all.

It feels good for me to look at the new ideas, currencies and methods of transacting that are coming our way.

It is like I am having a mindset shift and I am opening to the new ways of myself handling and transacting about money.

I know things are working out for me and my dream to get back on the land and get off the grid is coming closer and closer every day.

I had a hand and card reading yesterday and the lady said all is great, money is coming in and she said I will never have to worry about money next year. She said things will flourish for me. She also said that I am going to move, which is good and that an opportunity will come to me in about six months that will change everything for me.

I sort of feel I can sort it out now. The doubt and fear creeps in, though I know I am have the ability to change it and turn it around.

It is not a fact of I am going to do this, I AM doing this, right here and right now.

More positive discipline, focused action and passionate dedication.

I am off for a walk, to chant to myself to see my radiance shine.

5.40 P.M.

Things are moving ahead.

I keep showing gratitude each day saying the things that I am happy and grateful for.

I did a newsletter today.

I did my fifth Plant Thymes blog which is easy and great.

I sent my automated mail out and I got more sign ups.

My aim is to get 2,000 on my mailing list. I will give away the holiday thing soon. I look forward to checking that out.

The most valuable thing I have will be my email addresses. Here the aim us to get them in, so let us manifest that.

I have 50,000 on my mailing list which makes my life very easy.

This is 50,000 people that gives me a 12% to 40% that will only actually open up their emails, so this is about 15,000 people out of that 50,000.

If only 2% of the people sign up for what I have to offer, then that is 300 people that will buy my products or who will sign up for my program.

This is them signing up for the 'next thing.'

This makes my life so easy.

So universe, I love it when you send me new people who are signing up for my programs or my freebies.

I have two cheat sheets and two mini courses which I am giving away for free and people want to sign up for these.

I have a chapter to an e-book. What else can I give to entice people to sign up to my courses and programs?

Holidays, books, information, cheat sheets.

I will give it some more thought right now.

Day 51

Today I discovered that the more specific I am about what I want and the faster and the more charged the manifestations will be.

What I am excited to talk about. I want to talk about it.

I am eager to share what I have learnt and I will work the bugs out of the processes to make myself clear and content.

3.30 P.M.

I have just come home from a visit to a house, it is a B n B.

I was visiting a friend.

I am now in a bush block and after having a snooze I feel refreshed and frisky.

I wanted to come back and explore what I wrote about before.

I want to set dates to do my talks and I have not done so.

I listened to the law of attraction and I heard the words be more specific about what you want so here I am.

I want to do my talks to set dates to run these workshops. Let's change that.

The dates to my workshop are set.

Confessions of a Frustrated Business Woman

I am running one workshop a month and have two half day lead up talks. My dates are Nov 15th and Dec 7th. These dates are done.

The universe brings me the right venues for them. I have two dates locally and two dates in the city. I will also run the three day workshops locally and in the city.

It's great that I have this system in place. I create a systematic system for advertising. I look to pay someone $2,000 a month for a marketer and sales assistant.

Together we create a system that costs about $500 in advertising and the rest will be wages for my assistant. Here I am getting five to ten people in my monthly workshops and seminars. This will give me a 25% success rate.

The number that I will need for this is twenty eight people for the half day workshops. I will make it thirty people, and if I divide that by the four workshops, then it will be eight people will need to be there for each one.

This is what is going to happen.

People each half day and they all love what I have to offer. Things are working out for me now.

7.45 P.M.

Let me continued I got distracted by a phone call which led onto other things.

My participants want to have a more fulfilled life. They feel that something is missing in their lives.

They have everything though they are still hungry for more.

People come to me who know they will be best investing in themselves and to be able to make the changes that they want.

I ask the universe to help guide me to seeing what and where they are going.

It is all good and they also feel good. They are hungry for my practices.

173

So universe I am happy and grateful for my clients, I am happy and grateful for learning more about what it is that people want.

I am happy and grateful for the money that goes into my account.

I will meditate and see my radiance glow and glow.

The more I shine the lighter I become.

Day 52

I am sitting in the sun and it is lovely feeling the sun on me for a change.

It feels so nice, I am really enjoying it.

I have had two calls or texts or enquiries about my videos which is great.

I said to myself that I will start to livestream more and so I will. Two people have said "I have seen your videos" and they have commented on them. So I will definitely keep it up and will endeavour to do so.

I have my 144 topics and I have done eight so far and I will keep going forward with that and doing more. That will keep me busy for a couple of years. It is good to see and hear such feedback, and I appreciate that.

I give appreciation to the universe for bringing me new clients. I love seeing money coming in. I will also keep putting energy into creating more time for and doing what feels good.

It feels so good having the sun on my body.

I have had three clients book in now which is great. I am feeling great things are really working out for me now. I know consistency will really help out here.

I am committed at finishing my 144 topics.

I am consistent about bring change into my life. I am consistent about learning to be free.

I am committed to my visions to help change the consciousness of the planet. I am committed about changing for the better.

I am committed about having financial freedom. I am consistent about feeling good. I am consistent about growing my data base.

I am committed to bringing more fun and laughter into my life. I am committed to being free to be me.

I am committed to helping others to master their own lives. I am consistent about my divine desire to love and travel.

I am consistent about feeling healthier and happier every day. I am consistent about my dedication. I am consistent about bringing in the breath of life.

I am committed to feeling divine love flow through me. I am consistent about keeping my life real. I am committed about knowing there is more

Day 53

I am coming back from being away.

I feel a little overwhelmed as my son is leaving me next year and he is going to live with his father.

This is so hard and I am not ready for him to go yet, another year would be good, though it is what he wants and he needs time with good male role models.

He is thirteen and he wants to be with his brothers and father. I know that is the best thing for him, though I still feel sad and hollow about it. He is the last of a long line of being a mother for twenty three years.

My body feels yukky and I had someone ring me because my credit card had declined. Bastard. It sort of put me in a downward spiral.

I know now is the time to change my outlook and the feelings that I have of overwhelm about it.

I will do it here and right now.

I know that things are always working out for me.

I know everything will be okay and money is coming in and I know that I am able to support myself and I have the power and the ability to do so.

I know when my son leaves my financial situation will change and it will leave me with a bit of a void. With that is some steady income. I will fill up that void now, as it does bring me some fear when I think about it.

I release the fear I have.

I allow the fear to leave my body and for it to allow me to be comfortable and confident in what I am doing.

I see myself standing in my own space and being secure in my own energy.

I am safe and secure in all that is.

I appreciate my value and I appreciate my life, my abilities, my potential and my freedom.

Day 54

The sun is shining. I can feel it on my feet.

Yipee, bloody ee

I just had a client and I am aware of the difference in my energy and how I feel.

I feel my confidence is better and I feel I can see and feel more things when I do my healings.

I was aware of the gratitude and the positive thought processes that I used to help change how we feel, regardless to the filters and programming that we have.

I know that letting go of unresolved emotions is enhanced when we drop into our bodies and having conscious embodiment and creation.

Wow, that is a bit profound.

10.03 P.M.

I pretending today that the money I earned today was just pocket money. It is a sure thing and it means I am able to do something bigger and greater. There is always more!

I have continued with my business video series and it was great getting some response.

I have been away since Sunday and tomorrow is Thursday, so it is time to keep on with this journey.

The journey is of consistency. Of being on my journey of putting myself out there and sharing what it is that I have to say, sharing my message.

Persistence and consistency is the key.

I know that things are always working out for me.

Over time I have enjoyed this journey and I have enjoyed journaling what and how I do and I am sure I have said this time and time again, the best way to be successful in business is to bring happiness and contentment into your life. Do what you love and love doing it. I truly believe this now.

I have learnt that manifestations can take time.

It can be instantaneous and it does not matter how big or small it is. Small things can take time and big things can come instantly. It is all a matter of focus and then letting it go.

This means that changing being a long time in despair about your financial and state of business will take refocusing and consistent action to turn that around. Reprogramming my beliefs and though processes day after day and I believe this diary has proved this.

The Law of Attraction states that we have to line up and be a vibrational match to what it is that we want. Despair does not line up with freedom or abundance.

I have to be those things. I am free and I am abundant.

Bloody Nora, I hope I have not repeated that too many times now.

I have still avoided setting my dates for my talks, so I will be specific and talk about that.

I love talking to people, I love having an audience, I love having and audience.

I love sharing my knowledge.

When I was on the beach this morning I was seeing myself with large amounts of money coming in and the first thing that I said to myself was

"I imagine all the people I could help from doing the work that I do. I imagine all the people I could touch and bring healing into their lives."

I am a great speaker and I change people's lives.

I bring people epiphanies for change. I love seeing the light bulb moment come on for people.

I know that I am changing the world, one day at a time, one person at a time, one family at a time.

Day 55

Today is the first day in a long time, that I have been able to sit crossed legged.

I always loved sitting like this and then something happened to my knee. My knee just started to ache and be sore and when I would cross my legs it would hurt, a lot. I would have problems standing on it after sitting down.

So this is a great thing as my health is improving. I will sit cross legged once again.

I love it that my health is improving and that my pain at decreased.

I love feeling healthier and happier each day.

Talking of progressing vs digressing.......

I believe that I am learning to stay in my positive power and seeing and feeling the abundance around me, when others see suspicion, caution, crazy schemes, money scams, and ill researched action.

It is interesting how we can have different perceptions.

It is all about perception and how we see things. It has been shown now with science that is it how we perceive things that change our biochemistry and how we react or act to them.

Mmmmmm

So when we cannot change the things that are around us, we can change how we perceive things.

I have really worked and focused on bringing my present state to where it is now.

I earnt $445 yesterday, with a client which was great for one day's work. It actually ended up being half a day's work. I believe it was good. In fact it is bloody fabulous.

I believe I have manifested and created some great changes, so what can I do to keep the doubt at bay?

I can light incense and burn crap that does not serve me.

I can see myself in a mirror and be surrounded by golden radiance.

I can see the abundance all around, in the leaves, in the flowers, the trees, birds, in fact abundance is all around. It is around in the colours we see, the air we breathe and in the many bountiful things that this planet provides for us.

I can see the joys in the air I breathe, in the world everywhere.

I can acknowledge my own doubt in places and times when I doubt, when I doubt the word and integrity of others.

I can see them leave and go. I can see and them following their own journey.

I can see the doubters just falling away from me and disappearing into the ether.

I would like to write a mummy poem. I can talk it!

1.15 P.M.

I am pretty pissed off now.

I am fed up being brow beaten by others around me and who have different opinions to me.

It's okay to have our own opinions, though there is no need to bully others about their beliefs. Our individual beliefs are our own truth, not the truth.

There is no need to shove our beliefs down others' throats or make them see or believe what you do.

It sort of pisses me off when others do that.

It is disrespectful.

I will remove this energy from my body.

I will remove all the anger right here and now and I will see what happens.

7.15 P.M.

I am feeling a lot more settled now.

I have been busy tidying up and putting another course online.

I did my weekly recording and I am getting the hang of it now.

It takes time to learn how to run that mailing software, load videos up on you tube, write copy.

The more I am doing it the more proficient I am becoming.

As I have said before persistent action, persistent action.

Keep fine tuning and more persistent action.

Day 56

I had a very frustrating morning with other people's dramas and letting it affect me.

This has been a common occurrence in my life and I really could have an award for having been the biggest drama queen myself.

I have been more mindful over the last few years of walking away from dramas and not getting involved or attached to it. Cut the threads, pull out the hooks, cut the threads.

That has set me back about how I feel about myself, when some is telling you that you are not good enough. I have had that happen to me most of my life and I have had enough of listening to it now. I believed it in the past though I am not going to believe it any more.

I have noticed over the last fifty six days that I am influenced by those around me.

It shits me that I have to defend who I am and what I believe. I know I do not need to defend my honour. We are all free to be who we are.

I am sure this is what part of this lesson and learning gift is for me. It just does not feel good right now.

It can be hard not getting involved when people go out of their way to hook you into the game.

I know what I have to do and so I have to keep on keeping on.

It is imperative for me to focus on my journey and to be looking at giving myself what I need to feel secure, happy, abundant and free.

I have been called names and have been told I am obsessed, though when asking what would be a more preferable option, then there is no reply.

Maybe fingers are pointed at me because of others lack of focus and action with them.

The process is learning to know what is my shit to sort out is and what is not.

Anyway, that is all someone else's process and not mine.

I am focused on my life and my business and I see where I get hooked into others shit. I know that continual nagging and having others opinions put on me grind me down.

I am fed up of being ground down.

It is important for me to stay on top of my game. It is important for me, my family and my business.

For me to succeed I have to feel good.

I got up and I wrote, I meditated and I got into a great space.

This is the best practise I know to stay healthy and happy.

It is also no good not reacting when I am in the midst of a drama.

Time out is good.

I have to practise doing it when the waters are calm. When I am reactive, it is important to do something that will lift my spirits and will change the direction of my focus.

I know each time I am triggered it is more things to clean up and process, release or bring it.

It is all gifts and I do know that.

I think I will go and listen to some music or watch a funny movie.

Day 57

It's a good day today.

I had a run in the morning and then I went for a 10km bike ride and that was good.

This is the first time that I have had a bike ride in ages. I was very pleased about that, even if it made my bum hurt.

I did a livestream today, it was a rampage or a focus wheel about what things make you feel good. As I was talking about the things I like and that excite me I could feel myself becoming more excited.

The best time to do this and ramp it up is when we are feeling good.

I have spoken about the focus wheel before. It is a great way to focus and bring in into your life what you want.

Let us give it another go.

To refresh, in the middle of the circle you write down what you want.

Then you put twelve segments around the middle circle, like the twelve numbers of a clock. I am sure you can search an image of it on the web.

In these twelve segments of the clock you write down twelve

things that are true present tense statements. These are things that are real, that you believe in and things that are happy for you.

Here is my example.

My middle statement is

'I love having eight to ten clients each week.'

This is a statement of what I want, it is not quite happening yet and it is something that makes me feel a little squirmy, or a little uncomfortable.

My twelve statements are then as follows

1. I welcome this change
2. I know that things are always working out for me
3. I love paying my bill with ease
4. I love treating my family to good things in my life
5. I love having money for investing in the things that I believe in
6. I love having time for fun and good things in my life
7. I know I give value to people and I am valued for that
8. I know my radiance continues to grow each day
9. I love having holidays and adventures
10. I love helping others to feel happier and healthier
11. I love being pampered and having massages regularly
12. I know things are always working out for me

Day 58

I have a confession to make.

It has been a few days since my last entry.

Things are starting to change and grow. Maybe I do not need you as much in my life my friend, as I am not drawn to write about my frustrations and my failing business any longer. I am now filling my life with good feeling things.

I have been busy with business, woo hoo.

In fact I had three clients back to back yesterday. One tomorrow and then more after, I believe now.

My social media account was blocked today and it would not let me in. Not sure what is happening there, though I am sure it will always be for the highest and greatest good. Maybe it has been hacked.

It is a pain in the backside as I finally booked my dates for my workshops and to start my Higher Laws journey and I was ready to start putting up some event pages and to start advertising them.

Maybe I will have to go to eventbrite or sticky tickets and advertise them there. I have spent a good hour on it today.

Some of my financial investments are already starting to move and flourish. This is fantastic and I am very pleased about that.

I will write some manifestations about my block of land.

My block of land has lots of bush on it and it backs onto national park. It is a perfect block for us.

It has plenty of space to feel free and the bush block can just stay bush, no need to cut down any trees there. The bush gets used for walking the dogs and horse riding.

There is about ten acres that is cleared and is great for me to use for the chooks and sheep. This makes great compost to grow stuff for us to eat and drink.

We grow food and make our own wine. I love having a veggie patch and having the WWOOFERS (Willing workers on organic farms) here to help manage it and eat from it.

Our house starts off small and then increases over time as we have the time and materials to create and build workshop space, work sheds and studios. These extensions all accommodate for all our needs.

The love of my life also loves this space. We have created it and built it together.

He has his man's shed and I have mine. We also have a core space that we have built have together. We both love to build and to create things.

We create a space for workshops, for teaching and sharing our stuff. People are happy to come to us.

I run detox workshops, relationship workshops, transformational workshops, spiritual workshops, plus more. I do not have to organise them, it is all done for me.

My workshops revolve around

- Emotional and mental clearing
- The Higher Laws
- Detoxifcation
- Healthy nutrition
- Wholefood preparation
- Sustainable living
- Healing

- Couples and relationships
- Family unity

The list could go on.

All my participants pay happily and easily for the services that they receive.

I am changing lives.

I know they are feeling amazing.

I know I change people's lives. I know the ripples are spreading out.

The love revolution is here.

Day 59

I have one more day to go.

So much has been happening in my head today that I feel quite overwhelmed.

When I feel overwhelmed then I can start to worry about things.

When I start to worry about things this can knock me off my perch and it does not help me in any way at all.

This is how the cycle can start. I know it is good to nip it in the bud when it is early on in the cycle.

Then the stress sets in.

I sat in the massage chair and I could feel my body letting go of the stress. It was de-stressing.

It is important to keep myself in a good space.

It is important to take time to pamper myself, to focus on me, to do what feels good.

Money has been coming in and out, business is flowing in and out.

I have started to invest some of my income in new ways and I am now looking at dealing with money in a new way.

There are new opportunities coming to me now and I know this is because of the change in my mindset.

It is good being busy, though it can get overwhelming at times.

I could easily get lost in the rat race and the 'To Do's' and the 'Must Do's,' the commitments, the 'have to's,' and don't forget the 'want to's.'

The most important thing that I have to do is to stay keeping myself in a good space. I see my body radiating with joy.

I see myself alive and alert. I see my future unravelling in an exciting and happy way. I know that things are always working out for me and I am pleased about that.

I love clients walking in the door and ringing me out of the blue.

I love connecting with new people and then seeing the joy in their lives and teaching them new ways of living and existing. I love gifting people ways for them to be happy and to be connected to themselves, to their God and to the other people in their lives.

I see my radiance, I see the light shining. I know the more I see this, the more I clear the energy inside and the clearer I become, the faster and easier it becomes to manifest. Life flows through me.

I know it just takes one day at a time. Just one day.

One moment to be, love and have all I need.

This journal and diary is nearly done.

Will there be more confession diaries, who knows?

I hope this may inspire others to allow themselves to be the true radiant being that they want to be.

I also hope that this will inspire people to write their way through any problems that they have.

Remember the key is to acknowledge where you are at and then write about what you want to happen.

It will be great and things are happening.

Tomorrow is a new day, filled with great things and the most important thing is to laugh and to love myself.

So be it.

From now until next time and tomorrow,

I am no longer frustrated or wimpy when it comes to business and I can right the feelings and increase my value and let great business come in.

So be it.

Day 60

This is the last day of Confessions of a Frustrated Business Woman.

I was going to call this Diary of a Wimpy Business Woman, though I will go with the frustrated one instead.

I was feeling wimpy and now I am not.

I was frustrated and now I am not.

Job Well Done!

I was down and out about money and now I am not.

I was lost in focus and direction in my life and now I am not.

So I will boast about the benefits and positives that can be had from journaling and finding a friend in a diary.

Diary you became my friend, you helped me to share my trails and tribulation about supporting myself financially. You have been a friend and a sounding board for me. You have given me the space to share my concerns and worries about having to work with others concerns, worries, places, events and dramas.

This is priceless the friendship that I have had with you.

You have allowed me to monitor my actions, my thoughts and my beliefs and then put them all down on paper. You have also provided me with space to write about my business learnings and lessons.

You have given me a space to write about the things I am grateful for and the things I am happy about.

You have given me space to share about how I would like my future to look like. I know this diary works, it bloody works.

As I keep focusing on what I want, I know that I get closer and closer to getting there each day.

When I focus on my lack, I only find lack.

When I focus on my joy, I find joy.

When I focus on how it will be and feel good, then it happens for me.

Over sixty days ago, I was chasing clients and counting my money at the supermarket.

The last few weeks I have had at least five clients a week and I have not had to chase anyone. They are all now coming to me.

The most important thing for me to do is to feel good and to keep feeling good. I know I have repeated myself so many times, though this is the process, to keep re-affirming this and the power of writing is a powerful way to do this.

Seeing how I want my great life to be is a powerful thing.

This is not my only frustrated or wimpy diary. I plan to keep doing them for as long as there are areas in my life that I want to change.

I want my life to be a conscious co-creation. I want things to keep working out for me. So the practise is to be centred, connected and aligned. This is paramount.

The rest then just falls into place.

When I am worried and I am in a space of "Oh my God, what am I going to do?", then things do not come to me.

When I am in a space of 'things are always working out for me' and I day dream about how my life can be, things start to come.

Since writing this dairy I have engaged in activities that have made some big changes in my life and some new paradigms of thinking. This excites me.

I have started singing and dancing lessons.

I have connected with new people and have found common interests.

I have taken my focus from work, work, work to more play. I have changed my addictions and work did become one of them. This diary helped open my eyes to this.

I am now doing things that I love to do.

I have engaged in being happy and playful. I have increased my value and my self-worth.

I have been affluent and have let go of the struggle.

I have received some great things in my life and I appreciate that. Things are flowing in.

So I will keep on visualising and manifesting for old times' sake.

It will be important for me to be consistent with this flow of energy until it becomes habitual.

I love it when clients just ring me up and come and see me.

I love it when things are always working out for me.

I love feeling good, in fact there is nothing better than feeling good.

I know that things are always working out for me.

I know I have five to ten clients each week now.

I know it is easy for me to pay my bills and my mortgage.

I know it feels good to pay my bills easily.

I know life is fun and life is great.

I like to take my kids out and we like to have a good time.

I like to celebrate feeling good and having fun.

I like to buy whatever foods I want, when I want.

I know that things are doing well for me.

I know that I welcome good things in my life.

I know my tribe continues to grow and my following grows.

I know practise makes perfect.

I know I am happy and I feel good.

I know I am creating the life I want, just the way I want it to be.

I know my health improves more and more each day, in every way.

I know it is important for me to feel good.

I know it is important to be great and to laugh and play.

I know I love to have a good time.

I know I love to travel and play.

I know I love to help others.

I know I am a powerful healer.

I know my avatar.

I know that I look forward to more happiness that is coming my way.

I know I can keep doing this diary if I choose.

I know I can do this all again if I need to.

I know that because I have done this once I can do it again and again.

I know this diary worked wonders for me.

I know this can work for you.

Write down what you want.

Write down how it looks, feels, sounds like, smells and tastes.

Spend ten to twenty minutes doing this every day.

Then let it go and just be open to receive.

See the subtle differences and give gratitude for that.

Welcome the changes that are coming in and appreciate them.

This is the key, this is the work.

Enjoy your life and may your God/Universe/Source energy bless you.

Seeing you always in health, love and happiness.

AHo

Louise

Printed in the United States
By Bookmasters